Short

and

Sweet

Small Words for Big Thoughts

Some Warm
Some Wise
Some Witty

COMPILED AND EDITED BY

SUSAN KING

Broken Arrow, OK

Cheryl B. Lemine photo credit: Iman Bethel Photography

SHORT AND SWEET
Small Words for Big Thoughts:
Some Warm, Some, Wise, Some Witty

ISBN-13: 978-1-60495-027-4

ACKNOWLEDGMENTS

First, thanks to my dear brother, Larry Cheeves, who — even while battling a nasty cold — worked slavishly to help me organize/page this book and to his wife, Lori, who nurtured me through the last days — making sure that I had enough to eat and got at least a few hours of sleep each night.

Thanks also to Sue Rosenfeld (with Rosenfeld Communications and also a conferee at one of the writers' conferences) who, for over a year, sent me tons of enthusiastic emails filled with ideas for this book.

A special thanks to Tracy Ecclesine Ivie and her seven siblings for giving us permission to publish their father's work.

And finally, thanks to Terri Kalfas of Grace Publishing for taking on this book — our mutual labor of love.

TABLE OF CONTENTS

INTRODUCTION

It all started decades ago when Mary Lou Redding, who served for 33 years as managing editor of *The Upper Room* magazine, caught an idea from a professor at Fort Wayne University. Further inspired by Joseph A. Ecclesine's "Big Words Are for the Birds" (which begins on page 64), Mary Lou started assigning a one-syllable-word exercise in classes she taught at various writers' conferences all over the country.

For the past 20 years, when I have represented *The Upper Room* at writers' conferences, I have continued giving this assignment to those in my classes. These writers are all motivated to learn whatever I can teach them about perfecting their craft. They are more engaged than the Christian college students I've been teaching for over 20 years because they know they're going to apply what they've learned — not the day before the test or even next week, but probably within an hour after they leave the classroom.

Still, they have come with the attitude that we who love to write all share. After all, we're writers. We love words. If a few words are good, many are better — especially the interesting word, maybe the elegant word...and definitely the special word only a particular writer can use.

"This pen is being operated by a professional writer. Do not try this at home" is what we want to see at the bottom of every page we write.

And so we love to use the long, impressive words.

But that kind of word tends to work against good communication. The truth is, the best communication is what the readers/listeners understand with the least effort — a Mr. Spock mind meld as it were

— as if the ideas were just flowing from the writer's mind to theirs with no actual words involved.

"In the beginning were the *logos*, says the Bible — the idea, the plan, caught in a flash as if in a single word," writes Sheridan Baker.* This is the ideal: to capture the essence of our ideas in as few words, and as simple words, as the audience and purpose dictate. We may love words, but if we use too many of them and ones that are not familiar and comfortable to the average reader/listener, then words just get in the way. Writing tight (saying a lot with a little) and using crisp, clear, accessible words in our writing and speech bring joy to the readers/listeners even if they may not know why.

Actually, that's good news for any of us who long for others to understand us, to hear us. The words we really should be using most of the time are already known to us. We don't have to get a college degree to learn them; we just think that we do. So we all need to break our attachments to those multi-syllable aliens that even non-professional writers/speakers tend to favor and get back to the familiar words of our childhood, the cherished words, like "brave," "true," "loyal," "love," and "joy."

Hence their class assignment: In 250-300 words, write about something you care about, something that's important to you, using words of only one syllable, with the following five exceptions:

1. Any proper noun is okay. (Don't lie. If you were born in *California*, don't write *Maine*; if a name is *Machenheimer*, don't write *Clark*.)

2. You may use multisyllabic words of five letters or fewer — *into, over, area, about.*

3. You may use contractions of more than one syllable — *couldn't, wouldn't, didn't.*

4. You may use numbers (even those that are multisyllabic).
5. You may quote the Bible word-for-word regardless of one-syllable words.

The day I assign this homework, I see the reaction on the writers' faces, if not in their words: "I didn't become a professional writer to sound like Dick, Jane, and Sally."

These writers may have privately cursed me for this assignment (and definitely complained about it to my face later that day), but by the time they have finished it and return to class the next day, they are all so proud — and rightly so — of what they have written. When I ask for volunteers to read their assignment aloud to the class, nearly every single writer stands up to read.

Over the years, after hearing all the readings in class, several of the writers would say I should collect the assignments and publish them in a book. My reply? "What would be its theme — 'One-syllable words?'"

Well, guess what? At one such conference, Terri Kalfas of Grace Publishing stepped up to say that they wanted to publish just such a book. At that same conference, several of the writers expressed their enthusiasm for the project — a labor of love. Below is the response of one of those writers, Sue Rosenfeld:

> I've been thinking back to your class and what was shared there.
>
> I remember such a depth and breadth as we listened, took notes, wrote, and then wrote some more. We were not a group of hundreds in a large auditorium but a small group in a classroom each morning and around a lunch table one day who had developed just enough trust to be a little bit vulnerable with our words, hearts, and creations.
>
> Some of what flowed through us to each other in doing

the one-syllable assignment was serious; some of it was not. Sometimes a slight smile or quiet chuckle bubbled to the surface; other times hilariously funny and laugh-out-loud moments shot up like a grand old geyser. Some words invited deep reflection; some just let you be. Some stories revealed much; some revealed little. Some creativity was subtle; some was easily seen. All of it powerful in one way or another. All of it impacting us in that moment, in that place.

Now I am inviting you, dear readers, to share that place. The assignment is open to all comers. Just write your piece — conforming slavishly to the rules listed above — and email your submission(s) to shortandsweettoo@gmail.com. Soon, you could be seeing your own work featured in the next book in the *Short and Sweet* series!

~ *Susan King*

---

*excerpt from his book, *The Complete Stylist and Handbook 3*rd* edition*. New York: Harper & Row, 1984.

1

AND SO, I WRITE

I am a nerd. Not a math nerd or a tech nerd but an odd breed of nerd — I am a word nerd. You see, I love words! I love to see them woven into art with thread on cloth or with ink on paper or with paint on walls. I love to hear them ring out with lyric and tune, and I lift my voice with joy to match them.

I *keep* words, too. I save them on paper — on small scraps and on large sheets. Words hang in neat rows on the fridge or rest in a tray on my desk. They are filed in a box and also stored in the "brains" of that desk-top word-maker on which I type each day.

My love of words does have a limit, though. The line is drawn when I open my mouth to speak. The truth is, I am much more at ease with the words I *write* than with the words I *say*. At times, the words I *say* come out a bit dull or way too sharp or minus the pinch of wit I meant to give them. "Think first," is my motto; but I fight a daily war — on guard to halt the wrong words and let the right words pass. Sadly, many a fight has been lost for lack of just the right word.

And so, I write in full faith and trust that my words will bring good to those who read them.

Be it on scraps of paper, in books, with songs or through art — in all these ways, words give me a glimpse of their great power. They pull me and they push me in a give-and-take of pain and joy to merit all the best both sides can offer. The words I write take time to come forth; but to a word nerd, the labor is not in vain and the birth is well worth the wait.

Suzanne D. Nichols

2

THIS GOD

I stood at the top of a stark hill made only of hard stone with no plants and no soil to speak of. On that hill were crags and troughs but no flat place at all. Edges had been worn smooth by years of sun and rain. Not much was there to draw the eye or the mind. Yet I had longed to stand on this rock, not for its looks or its fame but for the words of a man who had been there at a time long past.

The small hill sits below one far more grand. On this tall hill stands a shrine to the she-god, Athena. In those years long past, it was the pride of this most grand of all the city states of the Greece of old. It was a light, a star that shone for the city of Athens. It showed the world the power and skill of art and craft in the hands of man. It was a gem. It was a raised fist.

His name, the man long passed, was Paul. He had once been a scourge to those who trod the way of Christ. But he "saw the light" and turned to serve the one Lord. So he had to go to Athens. As he walked the town, he saw a vast array of shrines and idols to every known god in the Greek realm. Then he saw one to a god they did not know. The Athenians did not want to anger any god that might harm them out of spite. Those who heard Paul's words took him up to Mars Hill, a place where the wise and sage of the City met to hear new things.

As Paul stood in front of them, I know (or think) he must have thrown his arm toward the shrine on the hill above as he said, "*This* God that you do not know does not dwell in grand shrines made by men. He is not served by the hands of men; in fact, He has no needs at all!"

He then told them that *this* God had made all there is and lives in all He made. He said all men will be judged by the man that *this* God raised from the dead. (See Acts 17:16–44).

I thought of all that as I stood where this great man of God had preached. The shrine on the hill now lies in ruin — the idol god long gone. This God that saw Paul on the small hill now saw me. He also sees all other hills in all lands in all this world and on all other orbs in the vast sky, all at the same time. No, He still does not need my hands. But He gave to me His life, His love, His joy, His peace, and a life with no end. He has asked from me only my heart, my soul, my mind. It is a deal that beats every other ever made. It is an offer to all — but only if they know this God.

Larry Cheeves

~ ~ ~ ~ ~ ~

My task, which I am trying to achieve is,
by the power of the written word,
to make you hear, to make you feel —
it is, before all, to make you see.

Joseph Conrad

~ ~ ~ ~ ~ ~

A GREAT BIG ART SCHOOL

When I was in grade school, I went to an art school once a week. Each of us boys and girls who showed good skills in art had been picked from a school in or near our town. I rode to the class on a street car. When I got there, I saw lots and lots of kids.

First we stood in line in a big hall for a long time. Then we moved to the class room, where they gave us tools we were to use to make art. We sat in rows in chairs in the big room, some of us high up, and held boards on our laps. When we first sat down we watched some boys and girls draw with chalk on big sheets of news print. They stood on a stage down front.

Week after week we would go to the school. And week after week, the day would start when the prof came out. He was in charge of art for all of the schools in our town. We all liked him a lot. In each class he taught us a skill we could use, and then gave us the theme for the day. Then we each tried to do what he said, while he came to our chairs and looked at our work. He would praise the best ones and tell the poor ones what else they could do. When we had been in that class for two or three years, we were put in a class in which we used big sheets of news print and paint. I went to this art school one day a week for four or five years. When we reached high school, some of us went to a class in a school for big kids.

Eleanor Richardson

Is Love Blind?

They say love is blind, and I'm not sure why. You see, the love that saved me saw me even ere I came to be. That's why I love the Bible verse that tells us, *"Before I formed you...I knew you"* (Jeremiah 1:5 NIV). With this verse, I have an image in my mind of me — resting in God's strong-but-never-harsh hands. In a voice so low, so kind, so soft, He speaks His truth into my soul.

As He spoke, I came to be, and by His Word I breathe the breath of life.

Love is blind only to those who choose not to see. But for me, I know I love since He first loved me.

Marilyn Klunder

~ ~ ~ ~ ~ ~

Broadly speaking, the short words are the
best, and the old words best of all.

Winston S. Churchill

~ ~ ~ ~ ~ ~

5

THE LAST BEACH TRIP

My heart knew it would be our last trip to the coast where we had spent many joy- and peace-filled hours over the last 30 years. Our first night of being wed was spent at the beach. In later years our six kids — each while still at a crawl — felt the sand, the salt air, and the waves. The years saw many walks, talks, sand digs, and beach fires. This last day we lay arm in arm close to sleep, our cover the moist air, sun, sounds, and sights we knew so well.

Like the waves I can feel tough or weak, large or small, safe or in peril. God shared these ocean traits to take with us as we faced the months ahead. The first months were full of meds, tests, and hope. In the tenth month after the beach trip, it was time for him — my so-loved spouse — to leave. In his face, the face that I knew so well, I could see that he was at peace — even as his breath slowed until, at the end, only quiet stayed.

In the years since, I find life akin to what the ocean gives me in an array of colors, power, depth, and always the joy and peace I saw God give Stan.

Pamela Groupe Groves

THREE STARS
OF STRENGTH

Isaiah 30:15 NIV

As I started my day, I thought of all the notes I've taken the past three days as I hone my skills to write and I asked God, "What if my kids saw these pages? What would they see?" He said, "They would see lots of words going north, south, east and west. They would read rich and wise words of life that would fill their hearts, and teach them to start with True North." As we drive through life, with every one mile of High - way that we find comes two miles of ditches. The High - way is indeed clearly marked, but the way isn't easy.

My kids would also see stars by my key notes. One, two, or three stars that rate how I felt the value of each was to me when I heard it. This is a mark to come back to and to camp out there for sure. Each star shouts the voice of strength from God, Jesus, and the Holy Spirit and draws us all.

I pray that the ones whom I bore — now young adults — and all their babes will one day set eyes on the full strength of these three stars through me. And I hope that the wise words they read will fill their sails to live each day by the Lord's great strength.

God, I pray your *words* — "in quietness and trust will be your strength" — over my kids. May the skilled pen of your Spirit be read through my notes and bring life and strength to carry them forward.

Sandy Aletraris

7

ONE NIGHT A WEEK WITH PIERCE

Pierce is a smart boy who loves his pets, school, sports, art, and books. He is ten, and his mom was my last child. I love Pierce; he makes life sweet.

One night a week he stays at our house, and each week we make notes on plans ahead. We can't wait for the fun day! By noon on the days he is to stay, he calls and we plan what he wants to eat, where we will go, and what show we will watch that night.

I know he will want pens and paper to draw his thoughts and dreams. He has a gift. Not long ago, he drew the sky — and won a trip! You see, he did not draw the sky from the earth's view; he drew it from the view of space. You looked through the stars; you caught a glimpse of the moon, and you saw the earth with a storm in the seas.

Some days the sun shines, and he gets his ball and bat and asks me to come watch while he hits the ball over the fence. As the day dims, I think about how the clock runs away with time: first the days, then the years. I don't want to miss any day that he wants to be here with us.

Not long ago, he brought a book to the house that he could not put down. How thrilled we were as he curled up to read with a big glass of milk. He told us how good the book was and that his friends also like to read. Since friends can make a huge change in our lives, I thanked God for these friends. If Pierce loves to read, he can learn all the days of his life.

I know God has a plan for Pierce's life, and I pray for him to grow in grace. I also pray that one day he will be a wise man who loves with all his heart.

Linda Finlin

~ ~ ~ ~ ~ ~

William Faulkner once said of Ernest Hemingway: "He has never been known to use a word that might send a reader to the dictionary." Upon hearing this, Hemingway replied: "Poor Faulkner. Does he really think big emotions come from big words? He thinks I don't know the ten-dollar words. I know them all right. But there are older and simpler and better words, and those are the ones I use."

~ ~ ~ ~ ~ ~

8
SKY

Each day I see a new sky — but every time it's a sky I love. Some days it glows big and turns shades of blue, pink, and gold. At times it is gray, and then it cries.

In its storm mode, the sky brings large clumps of gray wool that change into dark slate. Then it booms and shoots sparks. When its rain runs dry, the sky smiles down at me.

When a cold wind brings clouds, the sky turns them into snow that lays soft down over the earth and hides the ground.

The clear, cold night sky is dark blue with bright stars. Harsh winds blow on my face and freeze my nose.

White cloud tufts float on the breeze, and I see shapes come to life: fields, seas, hills, and, yes, men with beards!

But I see the best sky at the end of the day when the sun shares its prism of light rays.

Doris Hoover

~ ~ ~ ~ ~ ~

How can I know what I think
till I see what I say?

E.M. Forster

~ ~ ~ ~ ~ ~

9

WONDERFULLY MADE

Every life is a gift from God. Why? Each one of us is made in the image of God. From birth to final breath, every day of life is a gift from God.

We can't deny that human beings grow from the day the sperm and egg unite. A heart beats 19 days after that tiny human comes to life in the womb. Nine months later, a baby is born.

God made our human body with every organ we would need. Though only three pounds, our brain helps us think and learn. We have a heart that pumps blood through 100,000 miles of veins in every adult. Our lungs help us breathe. What we eat goes through a path to use our food to fuel our body.

God made eyes to see, ears to hear. We can taste, touch, feel and smell because it was His idea. From head to toe, our bones frame our height as we grow. Our legs help us stand, sit, crawl, walk, run and skip.

Arms and hands, legs and feet — we could not move or pick up items, write these words, open a book if we did not have these parts of our body.

Like our thumb prints, our DNA makes us who we are. It gives us our hair color and eye color, and other facts such as how tall or short we will grow as we age.

We have 10,000,000,000 cells that form our body. These tiny units of life make up our skin, every organ, and our blood.

Truly, we humans must be made by God. Why? God alone could make life with all its gifts.

Jan White

LIVE, LOVE, LAUGH

A merry heart does good like a medicine,
But a broken spirit dries the bones.
Proverbs 17:22 NKJV

When life hands you bad news,
When things go wrong;
You can shake, with weak knees,
Or laugh and hold on.

You can laugh, my friend;
Or else you can cry.
They both flush sad thoughts;
They solve the same *"WHY?"*

Tears can wash out some pain in our hearts.
Humor smooths the way to make fresh new starts.

Share what you feel.
Show how you care.
Tears can open the flow;
For laughs you can share.

Some things you should know about a good laugh:
It's good for your health — and that is a fact.

Laugh and you ease the force of blood flow.
Laugh at your stress. With deep breaths, watch it go.

Laugh, and you help your whole self to feel strong.
You may not be sick quite as much — or as long.

A shine in the eye,
A grin on the face
Can wipe away tears
And put joy in their place
And give your poor soul room to breathe in that space.

Margaret Lalich

For your born writer, nothing is so healing
as the realization that he has come upon
the right word.

Catherine Drinker Bowen

11

BEING A DEAR ONE

It was brown, white, tiny, and crushed. One small drop of near life — gone. The mama bird called and chirped at the loss of this thin shell, split to ruin. But did she have more tiny ones, or was this all she had? The nest was too high for me to see. For now, it was for this one she chirped — over and over. This dear one, gone.

God knows the pain of the wren, the pain of the dear one, gone. But He calls me and tells me — over and over — that what was not true for the wren could be true for me. The shell can be healed of splits too deep for words and then filled with life that knows no end.

Oh the joy of being a dear one — saved!

Bev Varnado

~ ~ ~ ~ ~ ~

*A writer is a person who cares what words
mean, what they say, how they say it.*

Ursula K. Le Guin

~ ~ ~ ~ ~ ~

12

THANKING GOD
FOR HARD TIMES

After three years, I was moving to a new base in California. I
had tried hard in the Air Force to get a chance to prove what
I could do. Now I had that chance. As I drove to California on Route
66, I felt good. But a day into my trip, fear took over as I viewed the
hard tasks before me. *What have I done?* I thought.

The job was far more than I could do. This was why I was open
to an offer to teach me more about God. I had to have a lot of help.
Could God give that help?

I found that yes, He could. Soon, He helped me learn how to be a
Christian and used me while I worked this hard job. I gave God all
the glory for the way He gave me the strength and power to face the
hard tasks with honor. I even got a medal for my work.

So, why thank God for our hard times? My reply is that God brings
good out of them.

In my story, God used this time of trial to shape me into a Christian
of strong faith. God wants us to have joy in our hard times, to trust
that good will come from them. *"Consider it pure joy,"* Paul wrote,
*"whenever you face trials of many kinds, because you know that the
testing of your faith produces perseverance. Let perseverance finish its
work so that you may be mature and complete, not lacking anything."*
James 1: 2-3 NIV

Richard Kehoe

LIFE ON THE BEACH

Shells. Shells. On the beach, in the sand, here, there, at my feet. Waves wash them in, toss them hard on the sand, then melt the sand and suck the shells back out to sea. Some, but not all. Some stay for a while, and some shells, I guess, never leave.

The birds watch with me — sea birds used to such sights, used to the toss of the wind, the fly and seek of their own lives, the waves and sand and shells that come and go, or stay.

The great sea rules them all. In their ways, they trust it. If they could, they would thank it. They just are as it gives them to be.

Not like me.

I'm not a shell. Not the wind or a bird, not a wave nor the sand the waves wash. And God's not the great sea, but He made us all. He made us, but not all the same. The sea and sand, birds and wind, shells and waves on the beach — He made them and gives them to be as they are.

And me. He made me. But the gift He gave me is not like theirs. The gift He gave me is hard and sweet: the gift of choice. To be as I will.

So I go to the beach to learn life in His will. I go to see His peace. Feel it, hear it, smell it, touch it. Wave-tossed, wind-blown peace. There I learn to trust and thank the One who made us all. Who washed us. Feeds us. Saves us. And lets us choose to live in His peace.

Kathleen Brown

14
My Mom

A long, long time ago in a place not far from here, a child was born. She was fair of face and her name was Marigold. She grew into a fine young lady full of grace.

One day, she met Bob, a good man she could trust. They fell in love, wed, and had two kids.

I was their first child. Then came a son. Mom and Dad taught us to be kind, to let go of hurt, and to laugh at our own selves.

Most of all, they taught us to love the Lord.

I grew up and fell in love. I, too, wed and had two kids. And so the gifts of life were passed down. Be kind, let go of hurt, laugh, and love the Lord.

Marigold.

My Mom first and my best friend for the rest of her life.

Deborah Sprinkle

Start writing, no matter what. The water
does not flow until the faucet is turned on.

Louis L'Amour

15

Now Is the Time for Love

Leon was a good friend and close to my dad's age. Each day he gave me smiles and kind words. His yard was next to mine. We would both dig and plant and share our hopes for new blooms. One day he said to me, "Will you help me break up this ground so I can plant these shrubs?" It was late in the day. "I don't have time now," I said. I told him I would come the next day to help him. That night, he died.

Emmie was my mom's mom. When I was young she taught me to sew and cook. Each day she gave me a hug and a kiss on my cheek. When she grew old I would brush her hair and wrap it up in a bun on top of her head. This made her glad. One day she said to me, "Will you fix my hair?" It was late in the day. I told her, "I don't have time now." I told her I would come the next day to fix her hair. That night, she died.

I have a gift that will not be lost; sweet thoughts of smiles, kind words, a hug and a kiss on my cheek. Leon and Emmie. They gave their love while there was still time. They are gone, but their love still lifts my heart. They taught me this…now is the time for love.

Anne Grant

16

BONDING WITH BOOKS

I love to read. Books have been my pals since I was a young girl. Back then I would spend hours in a big tree in my front yard with a book in my hands. The books I read taught me things, made me laugh, and took me to far off places (in my mind). Nancy Drew books were tops on my list of what to read. As a teen I read spy books by Helen MacInnes. I had fun as I would guess who was the bad guy that we thought was a good guy.

I went to law school for three years and spent my time on books which cost an arm and a leg and were full of big words. When I had kids, I yearned to read to them and share my love of books. I read out loud to them each night. At first it was Dr. Seuss then Goosebumps. In a blink of an eye the kids were teens to whom I read Harry Potter books. Now that my kids are out of the house, I have more time to read books just for me. Some are ones my kids have read and tell me that I should read. I now work to write books of my own. One day I hope a mom might read one of my books to her own kids. But she will have no books to read if no one takes the time to write them.

Alice H. Murray

AFRICA ~ DARK LAND

A dark place," you say? No, no, not once in twelve years did I think of it as dark!

By day I note the harsh, bright hues of the mart: gold brown skin gleams in the sun; dust and sand, soil, bare feet. Shouts of all who wish to sell their wares pierce the air, "Who will buy our rice and oil, our greens, goats or grubs, our corn and chicks, our shoes, and shirts?"

Moms with babes tied close and firm on strong, lithe backs, one child in hand, press through the crowd.

With pail on head they trudge the long miles back to the clean, neat home of sticks and mud.

Three stones guard the wood fire and hold the pots of rice and palm oil for the one meal they'll eat this day.

The yard swept bare with branch of palm yields lush fruits to munch. A bright green snake might hide in the leaves of the palms that line the lanes and streams.

Nor e'en at night did I think, "dark"!

Bright stars glow in the vast sky. The Cross of the South peeps through palm fronds. A huge, full moon smiles down on those who dance and those who drum; on those who clap and those who hum.

From hot plains, through thick vines and growth to cool snow capped mounts on the band 'round earth's waist, this land speaks to me of life and *light*.

Sarah G. Smith Lewis

18

My Three Moms

Most of us have just one or two moms, but God saw fit to give me three. My first mom died just as I was born. It was not her choice to leave me. My dad was more than sad; he was mad at God. He could not get past his grief. And he could not care for me with four more kids at home, so I was sent to live with a new mom and dad from our church. I stayed with them up to the time I learned to crawl. They would have liked to keep me with them for the rest of my life. But by then my dad had met and wed the one who would be my third mom.

Edna cared for me for nine months as I lay close to her heart. Norma gave me back, though she did not want to. Ruth loved me and taught me and cared for me for over fifty years. How I love these three moms of mine! How I thank God that each of them has had a part in my life.

Liz Kimmel

~ ~ ~ ~ ~ ~

To gain your own voice, you have to forget about having it heard.

Allen Ginsberg

~ ~ ~ ~ ~ ~

19

FEAR NOT

Be of good cheer! The Lord is with you! Be strong in His might! Fear not!"

Those words rose up in me at just the right time for me to feel them all. They calmed me. They stilled my heart. They drove fear far from me. I felt loved, secure and strong. No thing, no threat, no voice could keep me from the safe place I'd found in Jesus.

My life had been marked with dark storms, anger, fear, and doubt. Hopes of when and how all this might cease had all been dashed. Screams and blows were my daily food. Would there be an end to this hard road?

Enter Jesus — friend. My help, hope, home. My love. He took my hand and led me to His heart where I found peace of mind, calm water for my soul, and a light for my path. He gave His life so I could find mine. He gave His love for me to share with every other one. We all need that kind of love.

Since the day our paths crossed, I've not been the same. Each bad voice of my past is gone or at least not the one I hear. What I hear is the call of my love, His hand in mine, that leads me on to all I'm meant to be. This path is so much more than I could hope for on these holy walks we share. He gives and gives and goes on to give some more. His love has healed my heart and made me whole.

Sharon Fincannon

20
4/17/17

On one day

in my life

I ran a race

to be near

hearts full of love

from the world

and from you

for me

that day.

Don Lee

21

MUSIC, MY MUSE

It's been said that music can slip past the mind to seek its home in our soul. When it does, it will stir up joy, love, or pain; and we feel them again — even when we had put them away "for good."

Joy will fill up what we lack.

Love lays soft pads on the hard rocks.

Pain opens old angst we want to lose.

What else can do that?

We can't avoid it. "Music is in the air," said the Dad, "it's near us."

"I know. I can hear it," added the boy.

Can you hear it? When you are open to it, you will.

Ellen Cardwell

~ ~ ~ ~ ~ ~

What is written without effort
is in general read without pleasure.

Samuel Johnson

~ ~ ~ ~ ~ ~

22

Skunks Smell Bad

Skunks smell bad.

My house sits right smack dab on their main path. My dog has not yet learned to stay away from them.

A dog, fresh from a run-in with a skunk, is hard to deal with. He is in pain. He stinks. He must be kept out of the house. My top dog-met-skunk fix is called Nature's Miracle.® I soak the dog's fur in this stuff and the smell goes down by half or more quite fast. I keep a quart on the shelf at all times.

Don't get me wrong. The dog still stinks for six months. He still must sleep in the garage for at least two nights. He still must stand at least three baths with skunk soap. But, at least I can get close to him to quiet him.

Why so many skunks? In front of my home is a house that feeds cats and birds. In back of my home is a house with fowls kept for their eggs. Even skunks must eat.

At least they sleep all through the cold time of year.

Jane Reid

STRONG WORDS
(OR WORDS OF STRENGTH)

The air is full of words, high and low tones blend with loud and soft sounds in a buzz that ebbs and flows at will. Come close and you will hear the trite and the deep — joy, shock, and fears — as lives tough through words that fill our ears.

Though we can't see them, words shape our lives from day to day. We talk about the things to do and share what's on our hearts. Words bring cheer or hope when we are low and point the way when we are lost.

They can also send wounds deep into our hearts.

Life or death, good or bad — words are full of *sense*. It's up to us how we use them to bring strength to those near us.

If our choice is life, for us and those we know, the Word will be our source and strength, for from Him all life flows.

Kay Camenisch

ALL FOR GOOD

You meant evil against me, but God meant it for good.
Genesis 50:20 NKJV

Jail wasn't one of my goals, but still I found my way to the white-box cell. When God found me, I was lost, but He made me pure, then lit my path to preach the light. He made me look at who I was and showed me in His Word the man I could be. The Holy Spirit came into a new life, made a change, and struck a spark.

This was very new to me, but I rose into the call to reach the lost. God gave me a stand, when I stood for him. He gave me a word in my heart, "Go put it on the lips of those you see; let them taste my fruit so sweet."

God moved me to His great task. With all of us, He takes the rough and makes them right, sets the path for our lives. I am sure He laid out *my* path and made *my* way. My heart is with the man in bars and wire, in a dark place, in his dark heart. This is the man I serve this day. God made the call and gift to be and set His Word in my mouth. My choice to shift my world from jail to the big house is set firm. I now preach seven times a month. My heart is bright. These are the ones I care for, since I was once one of them. God used the bad for good. He can do this in the lives of each of us so we can always aim our hopes high above who we once were, way out of the reach of our past.

Eric Mueller

MOVES THIRTY AND THIRTY-ONE

This used to be so easy. Off we'd go — house-to-house, ship-to-ship, and base-to-base with pets and kids all new on the block. Over and over again. We did it 29 times, but those days are passed and it has been a long time since we've changed zip codes.

Here we have grown roots. We call this place *home*, not a tour of duty. This is where we live and love, with a rich mix of hard and happy times, made whole and held firm with the joy of the Lord.

Now, with no want on our parts, Alzheimer's has come to live here. It's such an odd time. As the light dims in the mind of the one I love, our home sees less and less of the "we" that once was us, and more and more of only me. Now this house has too many rooms, too much grass, and too many things up high for me to take care of. We need less space. Move #30 is here.

> Oh, Lord, I know You have been, are, and always will be with me. I know You will see me through this, but right now my head aches and my heart breaks as I sift and sort, purge, pass on, and pitch. My faith is strong; it's my trust that's weak. The road ahead looks dark with so many rough spots, and I'm afraid.
>
> Help me, Lord. Help me to be brave and stay at peace — sure of who I am and Whose I am. Tell me, once again, how this place is not my home; how one day I will make move #31 and go to be with You in a place You have made for me... and will be there with You for all time. Amen

I may not know when that day will be, but I do know that today two men and a truck will soon be here, and I am not ready. Pens and clips still peek out of that cup by the phone and too many jars still have no lids. The kids will be here soon, too. They'll help me choose which rug to keep and which towels to use in the new bath. I know for sure I'll leave the grill and kayak, but all of my books — each and every one of them — have to come with me.

I look out at the yard and have to laugh. It's a good thing I never found the time to plant that blue bottle tree....

Penny Hunt

~ ~ ~ ~ ~ ~

I begin to think the chief difficulty in
writing a book must be to keep out what
does not belong to it.

George MacDonald

~ ~ ~ ~ ~ ~

26

DANCE THE SHAG

(DANCE FOR THE REST OF YOUR LIFE)

I love to dance! I don't know if there was a time when I did not love it. When I feel down or sad, I can put on a song and dance, and soon feel great. This has been true for me as far back in my mind as I can go.

As a small girl, I would dance with my mom and sis. We would tap dance at times to a fast song. We would swing our arms and legs to the beat. It was hard to do this and not smile — or even laugh. To hold hands would be fun, too. At times, my dad would dance with us. He was not at home as much to dance with us, but he did his share. If a friend came over, we would ask him or her to dance with us. Many had not shared this kind of fun prior to that time. I'm sure he or she went home to tell Mom about this odd event. You might want to try this kind of sport and fun with your child or friend.

I teach a dance at my class three days each week. It's called the Carolina Shag. A boy and girl hold one hand and move to the sound of a nice beach beat when they shag. The count is one and two, three and four, five, six. Each one steps back on the count of five. The boy often leads the girl into a turn. Girls love to turn! When they take a class, they have to learn many moves. The more moves they learn, the more fun it is to do.

This dance is well known all over the state of South Carolina. In fact, it's our state dance. When you see a boy and girl do the shag, I feel sure it will make you smile and tap your feet.

Come to South Carolina and just see. I think you will like it. Give me some of your time to learn, and I'll give you a dance you can do for the rest of your life.

Kae Harper Childs

A scrupulous writer, in every sentence that he writes, will ask himself at least four questions, thus:
1. What am I trying to say?
2. What words will express it?
3. What image or idiom will make it clearer?
4. Is this image fresh enough to have an effect?

And he will probably ask himself two more:
1. Could I put it more sortly?
2. Have I said anything that is avoidably ugly?

George Orwell

An Open Letter to U. S. Military Wives

We glimpse you — at school-bus stops, in the store, as you pump your gas. We drive past you and don't even stop to think. We often miss your power and your grace as you serve America right beside us every day. You are a hero in our midst.

Your loved one is far away; your heart is with him there. Your kids are under roof; your heart for them is here. We ask you to serve in your local church, but do we ever stop to serve you?

Do you feel our love? Our awe? Our thanks? Too strong to show us any tears, you wipe them away alone. These tears — this water of the soul — show me a solid truth: you are a jewel. And you are called, for not every wife can fill this role.

So I write this note to let you know that you are in my prayers. When I see you next, I'd love to wrap you in my arms. But until then, I hope these words can wrap your heart: You are a song so sweet and strong. *You.* You hold America in your hands, for you give your man strength, and you keep your kids strong as you hold their hearts in yours. I will sing from the roofs where un-sung praise is due.

Thank you for all that you do — for all you give to this land I love. God bless you, and the U.S.A.

Joleen Graumann

JET LAG

God so loved the world that he gave...
John 3:16 NIV

A nd Operation Christmas Child lets me give all year to kids far and wide. So, month in and month out, my place looks as if Santa lives here, and my friend Jean (not an elf) comes once or twice a week to help.

We fill each box with toys and things to make a child feel glad and loved. Oh, my, the things we find to stuff a box!

Bears and beads, hats and gloves, pens and pads on which to write.

Cats and cups, balls and bells, kits of planes just made for flight.

Dolls and dogs, cars and cards, plus lights to help kids see at night.

Box by box, we filled 1,500 last year and blessed 1,500 kids. But, wait: OCC says that each box can reach up to ten more folks with the Good News. So, you see, we show God's love to the world, and since we do it all from here, we've not once had jet lag.

Dolly Dickinson

KEEP 'TIL THE END

When I was young, I did not think much about time. When there's ample time left, it seems silly to fret over lost ticks on a clock. I knew a young man once who took his own life and left only a poem by which to make his mark. It began with the line, "If I had a chance to live life again, I'd start it with you and keep 'til the end." The poem was a sad prize in lieu of the life he could have given, had he known the Giver of Life.

As the years flew by and the blush of my youth gave way to the creased brow of a young adult, the days and hours seemed to speed up and rush by, but still I gave no real thought to the time I spent or the time I had left.

Now that I'm in what they call the prime of life, the end of the race has come into view, at least in my mind's eye. Though it's still hazy, I can see at last how short the race truly is, and it makes me value time as dear. This is not out of the fear of death or a want to cling to the time left here on earth, but in hopes that in my life to come I will be able to say that not one work carved out for me, not one plan meant for me, not one soul sent my way for love, care, or truth will be left on my bill. When I first met my Lord, and I gave my life to Him, I often wished that — as in that poem — my start had begun with Him. But now I know it's more vital to just keep 'til the end. When the last grain of my time on earth sifts to its end, I want to run into the days to come and know that I have served my Lord well and done so with all my might.

Annette Griffin

Time for Bed

I'm in bed, Dad," each child calls. My chores cease. Shows turn off. I take my eyes off of me.

"I'll be right there."

Room by room I go. "Did you brush your teeth? Did you wash your face and go pee?"

A book is read or a tale told. They learn this and will do this one day with a child of their own. I try to get it right. My mom read to me. My dad and I prayed. Yes, I try to get it right.

Each child is a gift, each one a world of dreams. Like seeds cast on soil, these dreams float in their hearts. Now is time to sort, to clear, or to save these dreams. We sort them in prayer. We take the day's joys, the tears, and the hopes to the throne of Him who sets our paths, who hears our cries, who grants the hopes of our hearts.

I give one hug, then two. I give a kiss and share a deep gaze so that the soul of each child knows what love looks like. Oh to show just a glimpse of the love God has for each of them!

My work is on pause; this is worth it. The show can wait; this is worth it. My dreams all fade; this is my dream.

"I love you, Dad."

"I love you too. I love you too."

David Alan Shorts

THE LIFE OF A CAT

The sun is up. Time to wake *her* up! How shall I do it today? Step on her face? Claw at her leg? Jump on her head? I know! I'll pull her hair.

Now is the time to duck! Here comes the swing! Whew. She did not catch me. At least she's up.

Oh boy, Oh boy, Oh Boy! I see the food. I smell the food. It's in the bowl. 'got what I want so no need to eat now. Back to bed. I'd love to go out, but first a nap.

There she goes. I'll miss her. But with her gone, I can get that dumb bird today! He steals the wire from the screen for his dopey nest, and I know my fierce growl will scare him away this time.

He'd best be glad for glass in front of me, or it would be bye, bye, Mister Wren.

Oh great. As soon as I scare that dumb bird away, here comes that randy tom. He riles me up like no other! I'll hiss, and I'll spit and show him who's boss.

If it were not for this glass, I'd take him out!

Oooh. The sun is out. The hot rays hit that spot on the floor just right. Now, I'll just close my eyes for a bit....

I hear the door. She's home. Did I doze that long?

Sure there's still food in my bowl, but I need her to put in more. Let me yell it to her. After all, she doesn't hear well.

As usual, she is glued to the boob tube. How 'bout I stroll in front of it? Whoa! Got out of the way of that shoe just in time.

Okay, now for that lame phone.

What? She is all about cats on the web! Hey, here — in your own house — a cat!

But wait, what's this…a belly rub?

Since I'm here and safe, I'll just close my eyes for a bit….

The sun is up!

Ah, the life of a cat.

Sharon Atwood

~ ~ ~ ~ ~ ~

Prowling about the rooms, sitting down,
getting up, stirring the fire, looking out the
window, teasing my hair, sitting down to write,
writing nothing, writing something
and tearing it up...

Charles Dickens

~ ~ ~ ~ ~ ~

32

HUGS

I love to hug. Cheek to cheek, chest to chest and knee to knee. For me, this is the right way to do it. If you like side hugs, I am not your girl. Through my hugs, I get to show you how much I care about your peace so just rest in my arms, breathe in and breathe out, and allow me to give you a break from the noise.

This is our time to know that "alone" is not in the cards for us. I am your friend and I'm here for you. Close your eyes if you need to; rest your head and let me hold you until you feel less sad, until you feel safe, until you feel loved. Stay here as long as you need to. I have the time.

In this hug, know that God *sees* you. My arms are His, and He led your feet to me for a time such as this.

When we let go, know that I wish you well, friend. I pray that our hug is with you the rest of your day. Head into those hours with a smile upon your face and light in your heart. Bring our hug to the next friend in need. Hugs can save a life, and we just may end wars with each hug we pass on. Hugs are the best.

I pray you know a life lived from one hug to the next, all your days.

Michelle Ruschman

Light Will Come

When gloom hides my way, I pray. For when I pray, light will come.

If my knees bend in awe and my hands rise in praise — light will come. If my eyes glance to the hills and my heart pants for the Lord, it will come.

By and by God hears my tears and calms my fears. I hush for the sound of His "still small voice."

But not this night. Bang! Flash! The great "I Am" sends a bolt of light! My feet find a lamp and my path glows white.

"Let there be light!" He shouts my name! Let doubt and fear, gloom and doom fade and wane down some black hole.

The light floods my soul. I see; I see! Praise God, I see!

So I trust these words: When you ask, when you seek, when you knock, and when you pray — light will come. Light will come.

Cureton L. Johnson

~ ~ ~ ~ ~ ~

I can't write five words but that I change seven.

Dorothy Parker

~ ~ ~ ~ ~ ~

34

THE WELL I DRINK FROM

Works of art lift me high. I see and hear and touch what a dream has birthed. Land and beast and man seized in bronze and clay. Paint on paper, wood, and cloth tell of life through the lens of the one who dreams. Words from the stage say what I can't but wish I could. I tuck them away for use later. A vivid photo makes me want to crawl inside. A film, large-as-life, looms over me with drama and story. And dance – when the body speaks in lines and shapes. I bask in the music of a choir that is also a flock – who sing in the tones of Zion.

When I drink from the well that is art, I too am part of a clan. In a white box of a room where works are hung or a dark box where an actor plays out life — and other art forms too — we fans bond even if we aren't aware. We each smile at the odd or just plain funny. We scratch our heads over what is called "mod." What makes my heart ache or skip a beat does the same for most. Art is the twine that joins us, and I don't have to know the names of those who sit or stand next to me.

When I need to break free from the usual, art paves my path. When I am lost; the right word, song, or scene morphs into my North Star. I find truth in the most small of things. I am filled. I flow over at times. A spring in my step is hard to hide. But know this: The way these things touch me all pale to one other way.

The drive to create moves me most. The brave ones with the gift plod on in the face of harsh odds and money woes. The phrase "you can't" falls away when the heart says "you must." Those who have the dreams never give up. Each and every wall, they scale. This is called hope. When I see hope in action, it speaks to my soul. I come alive. My stance is firm. I find the grit, the spark, the spunk I need to face what's ahead. I can begin again.

Kenneth Avon White

~ ~ ~ ~ ~ ~

It is no good starting out by thinking one is a heaven-born genius — some people are, but very few. No, one is a tradesman — a tradesman is a good honest trade. You must learn the technical skills, and then, within that trade, you can apply your own creative ideas; but you must submit to the discipline of form.

Agatha Christie

~ ~ ~ ~ ~ ~

35

As God Hems

You hem me in, behind and before,
and you lay your hand upon me.

Psalm 139:5 NIV

When I was small, our house was near two streets. Mom and Dad put a fence 'round our swings to keep us from the streets. I would swing and watch kids run from yard to yard. I felt as if I were in a trap.

When I had kids, I saw what my folks had done. One time our girls were in the back yard. I eyed them through the door. As I did the wash, I took my eyes off them one sec, and they were gone. I ran to the yard, full of fear when I could not find them at all. As I ran into the house, the phone rang.

Our house was on a road with two more houses. The call was from the gal up the road. The girls were there. I ran out of the house and up the road. When I caught my breath, I gave them each a hug. They were safe. It was time for joy — but their fence was on order.

As the sun set, I called my mom to thank her for her care to hem me in as a child. Then as I put my head down to sleep, I gave God thanks for His hem and hand on me — for the way that He has kept my heart and life safe from the harm of the world.

Tina M. Hunt

36

GOD AND MOM

I grew up with a mom who told me that she had trust in me. I would hear this often when on my way to a show or a dance with my high school beau. As sweet as that may sound, it is also a large load to drag through life. I didn't want to let mom down. I didn't want her to think less of me. I didn't want to hurt her or cause her grief.

We are both much older now; but the rules, and what she hopes for me, haven't changed. Through my life, those words have rung in my ear. I feel that year-after-year I have had to be on guard of what I did and said. That is big! I have viewed all things that have lured me by how mom might react if I did them or said them in front of her.

That kind of core debt means I must pray that God puts up His shield and stands with me as I go through each day. It is the same shield that God stood behind with David, while he put the stone in his sling to hurl at the giant, Goliath. As God was with David, He is also with me. Mom and God both had trust in me when I was 16, and they both still do.

I know that God hears all that I do and all that I say, and in time, so will my mom. My soul is strong in my faith in God. My heart is filled with His love and His will for me. My prayers are a plea to the one true God to not let me break the trust that my Mom, and He, have in me. I want to be a woman of faith — in my words, my acts, my heart, and my walk.

Toni Armstrong Sample

THIS KIND OF FAST

This kind can come out by nothing but prayer and fasting.

Mark 9:29b NKJV

Some evil only leaves by a fast.
Slow start:
Media
Sugar
One lunch
Two meals in a row
Hours here
A day there
Matthew Six

When you fast, do not look somber as the hypocrites do,
for they disfigure their faces to show others they are fasting...

Matthew 6:16 NIV

Learn
Value
Months pass
Hard
Heavy
Stress
Angst
Drain
Does God hear?

Head aches
Blood sugar low
Edgy by day's end
Yell at my kids
Count hours
Works
Not this way
How then Lord?
Guide me

Ephesians 5:15-21:
Use care. Think pure.
Walk best. Guard time.
Avoid evil. Be wise.
God's plan. Know Him.
Holy Spirit. Sing praise Psalms.
Be with Christ's kids. Think on Jesus.
Quiet with Him. Thank.
His order. Honor Him.

Jesus bids me,
"Come away!"
New view
Joy
Want
Eager
Full
Peace
Trust

Is not this the kind of fasting I have chosen:
to loose the chains of injustice and untie the cords of the yoke,
to set the oppressed free and break every yoke?

Isaiah 58:6 NIV

Huge news
Shock
Grief
Not my plan
Hard
Yet good
Bonds break
Stone heart melts
Only God!

He heals the brokenhearted and binds up their wounds.
Psalm 147:3 NKJV

Jennifer Saake

TREES...WHY DO I LOVE THEE?

Trees are God's gifts to the world. Their limbs reach up to touch God's face and host fruit of every kind — sweet pears, purple plums, figs and nuts and acorns that grow on stately oak trees.

A tree is made of bark, limbs, roots, a green leaf or two, buds and seeds. Trees give shade and block the hot sun, storms, winds, and rain.

Spring, fall, ice, and cold give trees a new coat of many colors. Red, gold, brown and green are only some of the many new shades.

Pine cones and the deep scent of the sap fill the woods with the joy of the pines.

Trees give us wood to house us and a place for birds to nest and rear their young. Trees give us logs to craft a fence to keep man or beast in or out, logs to make a boat and oars, and logs to build a raft to float far away.

Some trees give sap for sweet gum or syrup for our grits.

Trees may be used as good gifts for us, or they may be used for evil. A tree was the tool men used to craft the cross that Jesus was hung on. Jesus had no sin, yet some men did not like Him. Our lord had no sin, yet men took Him up to hang Him on the cross made of wood.

He who knew no sin gave His life on the cross for you and me. But was it evil? In some ways, no. For in God's plan to save our souls, Jesus had to bear His death on a cross to save our souls. From a tree came the cross where Jesus bled and died, but it was so we may live on. Such a huge price Jesus paid to save your soul and mine!

Pamela K. Proudfoot

THE JOY OF GOOD HEALTH

I learned to surf at the age of 46. I learned to ride my bike on trails at 50. I did my first Tri at 51 — just the swim part. It might not seem a great feat if not for this: These tests were all after my back went under the knife three times in three years.

I learned that to have health joy I must be wise. Every bite I eat and drink counts. All white food makes me swell, and ache in my joints. To have health joy I must ask: *What makes me feel good? What makes me feel bad?*

Good, deep sleep helps me to heal. To sleep on the couch or in a chair doesn't. Early to bed, early to rise is best. My friends laugh at my early hours. But it's how I fit in more book time.

Health joy is not just about my body; even more, it starts in my mind. If I carry guilt or walk in fear, it wears on my body. God's first plan was that I walk in peace. Left to my own ways, I will thwart that plan. I must shun fear, guilt, and worry that clash with peace and grow only weeds. Weeds that prick. Weeds that take over.

I choose mercy, love, and faith. Small picks, large gains.

When I work out, eat right, sleep well, I have the joy of good health. I get rid of fear, guilt, and worry to keep the weeds at bay. As I take in and give out mercy, love and faith grow peace that feeds my soul. And that can also yield life to my friends and kin.

Kimberly Long

40

A DAY WITH CHAMP

The sun's first rays hit Champ's face as he lies at the foot of my bed. Red and gold coat, big and soft with a long fanned tail — he tells me it's time to meet the day with the stare of his black-lined eyes. He waits, while I wake.

"OK Champ. Let's go." Side by side we walk down the stairs. Two scoops of food fill his bowl. Chunk, chunk, chunk, he eats it all.

"Come Champ, it's time for a walk." With glee he runs to find his leash. A thrilled pup, he knows where we are bound...our place, the park. I ride my bike with Champ next to me. The wind blows through our hair, his leash clutched tight in my hand. We pick up speed as we near the plush grass under the wide blue sky. I let go of Champ's leash so he is free to sniff and chase birds. I'm glad to ride ahead and wait for Champ to catch up to me.

He finds me for a race. We catch a glimpse of each other's eyes and feel free with flight. "One more time, Champ," I say as we turn on a knoll of grass to come back once more. Four, five, six times and we are done. "Time to go home," he says with his long stare. He trots home, too pooped to run.

Home again, Champ laps cold water. He finds his cool spot on the tile floor to lie on his side, arms and legs stretched out. He shuts his long-lashed eyes, breathes one more sigh, and sleeps. I like to think that he dreams of a day in the park with green grass, warm sun, wind in his hair, and birds to chase.

Rosie DiBianca

41

A LOOK AT FAITH

Joe's post read, "I learn day by day to let the space where I am and the space where I want to be serve to rouse me and not to bring fear." I wrote the teen back, "I think that space might be called faith." He liked my thought with a "thumbs up." And I dared to think it wise as well.

Faith comes as a choice in life. But fear and pain are not a choice. They will come to all. So it is up to us if we choose faith to face the fear and pain of life. Some may see no point in faith. *What's the use? Fear and pain are here to stay. Why have faith?* But for me, that *is* the point.

Faith brings peace through the toils of life. In fact, it can bring a peace that is not like the world's peace. Fear tends to be more of the way of man; I know that. But fear that lasts has no place in my world. My faith comes from the One who gives it. God is that One. He gives it to each of us in a size that fits. It's not one size fits all — it could be a small size or a large size. It is His gift to us.

One thing I learned is that when I use my faith, it grows. The more my faith is used, the more it grows. Don't get me wrong. I'm not fond of fear and pain, but I do like to grow in faith.

The Good Book says that faith is what is hoped for, the proof of what is not seen. By faith we know that the world was made by God's Word, so that what is seen has been made from things that are not seen. (Hebrews 11:1, 3 Author's paraphrase) That's what it says, and I have no qualms with that. It brings joy to my heart to know that God is there. He was there back when, and He is still here now. How do I know this? He is the great I Am — the One who sees all, hears all, knows all, *is* All. In that case, all I need to do when pain and fear show up is to trust in the great I Am. My trust will test my faith as it should. I lean on the God Who takes my cares from me, which leaves no room for the fear and pain that tries to take over my thoughts. At least that's what I make of it. And here's the sweet part. When my faith is full, it brings rest. Sweet, sweet rest.

Karen O. Allen

~ ~ ~ ~ ~ ~

I keep six honest serving men
(They taught me all I knew);
Their names are What and Why and When
and How and Where and Who.

Rudyard Kipling

~ ~ ~ ~ ~ ~

BIG WORDS
ARE FOR THE BIRDS

Joseph A. Ecclesine

When you come right down to it, there is no law that says you have to use big words in ads.

There are lots of small words, and good ones, that can be made to say all the things you want to say — quite as well as the big ones.

It may take more time to find the small words — but it can be well worth it. For most small words are quick to grasp. And best of all, most of us know what they mean.

Some small words — a lot of them, in fact — can say a thing just the way it should be said. They can be crisp, brief, to the point. Or they can be soft, round, smooth — rich with just the right feel, the right taste.

Use them with care and what you say can be slow or fast to read — as you wish.

Small words have a charm all their own — the charm of the quick, the lean, the lithe, the light on their toes. They dance, twist, turn, sing — light the way for the eyes of those who read, like sparks in the night — and stay on to sing some more.

Small words are clean, the grace notes of prose. There is an air to them that leaves you with the keen sense that they could not be more clear.

You know what they say the way you know a day is bright and fair — at first sight. And you find as you read that you like the way they say it.

Small words are sweet — to the ear, the tongue, and the mind.

Small words are gay — and lure you to their song as the flame lures the moth (which is not a bad thing for an ad to do).

Small words have a world of their own — a big world in which all of us live most of the time (which makes it a good place for ads, too).

And small words can catch big thoughts and hold them up for all who read to see — like bright stones in rings of gold.

With a good stock of small words, and the will to use them, you can write ads that will do all you want your ads to do — and more, much more.

In fact, if you play your cards right, you can write ads the way they all say ads should be done: in words like these (all the way down to the last one, that, is) of just one syllable.

Joseph A. Ecclesine was a Madison Avenue copywriter in the *Mad Men* era. He originally wrote this piece in the 1960s for other copywriters under the title "Big Words are for the Birds."

A shorter version, directed at the general public, ran in *Reader's Digest* and was titled, "Words of One Syllable."

These two versions have also appeared in *The American Journal of Economics and Sociology* and various other publications, while being used as inspirational models for college writing courses around the country.

Born in Boston, Ecclesine graduated from Fordham University in 1929, months before the stock market crash that triggered the Great Depression. He was fortunate to find work at the *Bronx Home News* during that period. He later worked in the press department of NBC in Manhattan, where he met his future wife, Margy, also a writer there.

They celebrated more than 50 years of marriage and had eight children. While living in New York, he worked at several major ad agencies and became promotion director of *Look Magazine*.

His catchy headlines and prose could be found in the campaigns of numerous companies, including IBM, National Geographic, Revlon and American Airlines. He also wrote fiction and essays, with a 1930s piece in *Esquire* magazine, followed by work in *The New Yorker, Newsweek* and *Short Story International*. He had an innate curiosity about everything, which translated into an extreme zest for life.

An accomplished watercolorist, Ecclesine allegedly sold his first piece to boxer Gene Tunney, who held the world heavyweight championship in the late 1920s. Ecclesine's watercolors were featured in *The Artist* magazine, and he had a one-man show during his retirement in San Diego. While living in California during his final years, he taught courses in memoir writing for senior citizens in a continuing education program at UCSD (University of California at San Diego).

43

AFRICA'S GRIP

In Liberia, we land in a sea of fog. Gas fumes fill the air as we wait for our bags. My team is here to serve dads, moms, boys, and girls. War has left this place in need. Soon Liberians greet our group with hugs.

Our clock is a farm bird's screech. At dawn, we see black smoke near the guest house. Peace time in Liberia means that these fires were set to clear land to plant crops, not to raze huts. Trees, weeds, and grass glow from the burn off. The rest of Camphor Mission Station looks like a Boy Scout camp: an open field with paths that lead to the church, health rooms, a school, and homes.

After lunch, the boys pick me up and walk with me to their blue brick school. They know I have a skill to share as we stroll to the end of the dark hall and face a locked door. Books are in there; I turn the key. They want to read to me. Our goal is for the kids to read these books each day. A three-year plan, so far. Soon Mary comes to greet me, and I will train her. She will make sure that the door to the book room will not shut out any child after I leave.

At dusk, we hike back up the trail; a white egret scoots past to catch bugs. I hear the squeak of the pump; the boys run for their baths. A whiff of char just like the aroma from our grills at home lets me know that the rice is ready. Our team will have much to share over this meal.

I feel as if I need Africa more than she needs me. Liberia has a grip on me.

Kevin Louise Schaner

44

More Than the Sum of Two

She came in the dark of the night. Her loud cry and strong heart said, "All is well." Her thick black hair fell past her ears and her blue eyes looked at mine. I raised her to my breast, this fresh, new life I now could see.

She was more than the sum of two. She was a work of art — a work that took nine months to weave. Those months taught me how to wait and pray and hope. God birthed in me a love so deep that I now know more of the depth of His love for me.

Karen Condit

~ ~ ~ ~ ~ ~

The difference between the almost right word and the right word is really a large matter. 'tis the difference between the lightning bug and the lightning.

Mark Twain

~ ~ ~ ~ ~ ~

45

GIFTS FROM GOD

My greatest gifts from God — my wife and boys — bring me no end of joy.

Jan loves music and shares my call to serve Jesus in the local church. She stands at my side to love and cheer me on, even at great cost. Her trust and pride in me are worth more than I can tell.

My dear sons, Ian and Mark, share few likes or traits. Ian hunts while Mark checks the music scene on his iPad. Ian grabs our focus while Mark waits for a break. Mark never speaks until after he thinks, but Ian thinks out loud.

Both work hard at the things they love. When not on the drums, Ian scours the area to snap an image with his Canon. Mark edits video and stacks cups. They both strive to be the best they can be.

Troy Dennis

~ ~ ~ ~ ~ ~

The most valuable of all talents is that of never using two words when one will do.

Thomas Jefferson

~ ~ ~ ~ ~ ~

46

WHAT BRINGS ME JOY?

What brings me joy in life? To help those who lead to use their strengths to meet goals and dreams. To equip them to seek new ways to shape the world — not just alone but also with the wealth of gifts each has. When we are kind and learn to care more for those we lift up, all will reap the gain. Our hearts and souls will guide us to do the right things, for the best group, at the choice time. As we coach and plan, we can clear the paths to bridge gaps for the next set of heirs fit to lead. We are wise to trust in their skills and teach them ground rules to live by.

The best place to show our hope and faith is with the ones with whom we share dreams. As we smile and laugh, we can spur them on — guide the hearts and minds of the new groups to do what is right. At times, we have to adapt to new ways so we can show how much we care. If we point those above us and next to us in the ways to win, then we win as well. As we use our trust in God to teach and train, we fuel a fire in those who will come next to search for strong plans to lead well. Our goal is to act now, to spark the next phase. If we have done our best, our new teams will lead well.

Dr. W. Alan Dixon, Sr.

Devotional in One Syllable

Read Matthew 5-7

Seeing the multitudes, he went up into a mountain:
and when he was set, his disciples came unto him:
And he opened his mouth, and taught them.

Matthew 5:1-2 KJV

Jesus spoke to those on the mount. He said that all who wish to could walk His path, live His way, and be blessed.

We should, of course, read what He said so we will know the words He used, and so we will know what He meant as well as what He said…such as that evil thoughts are just as bad as evil deeds.

He told us not to fret over what is said or done by those who are not of us, nor over what we will eat, or drink, or wear, or where we will live, for God knows what we need, and will see that we get it if we will walk His path and live His way.

More — and this is not all He said, or the real words He used — we are to love all, even if they have done us wrong; we are to do good works, even if no one else knows we do; we are to pray for those who harm us; we are to trust only in God, and not in man; we are not to judge or have ill will for any one; we are to bring our wants to God in prayer.

God knows our needs, and Christ showed us how to pray when

those who are His asked Him to (Matthew 6:9-13). On that same mount, He taught us to treat all as we would want them to treat us; and not to heed the call of those who would have us tread a path that is not the way of Christ.

Prayer: *Lord, you have shown us your way; please help us to live it. Amen.*

THOUGHT FOR THE DAY

Jesus taught me how to live.

Joseph Yates

So the writer who breeds
more words than he needs,
is making a chore
for the reader who reads.

Dr. Seuss
(Theodore Geisel)

48

I Miss Her

Most days she is happy to see me. "Can we go out to lunch today?" she says. We eat at the same place as if it were a first for her. "The light bulb in this lamp is burned out," she says each time I come. I plug it back in for her. "I would like a radio." From under the bed, I pull it out. She cries when she doesn't know what she has done or where to find her socks. I am sad and worn, but I do not let her see my pain. My visit brings her such joy. "I love you so much," she says. She tries to put on a brave face.

Only some days is she sad; those days she tells me she wants to die. I want to help. I hug her and try to talk about new things. She still loves to laugh and make jokes, so I can tease her, and she will soon laugh. I laugh too, but not in my heart.

I miss her, even though she is still with me.

I used to get small peeks of the lady who was my friend, and my heart would cling to them. Now the mom I once knew is hard to find. Bit by bit she has left me.

Tears wait for me at home.

Katherine Rice

Good News

God made us and gave us news to spread —
That Christ laid His life down, but He's not dead.
He called us good and planned our days.
He'll change us, in His time, His way.

As we share His Word, live freed from sin,
We can praise His name and give all to Him —
The One who is, who was, will be,
He stays the same for all to see.

Christ is He, whose love is deep.
He lives for us. We need not weep.
Loved face-to-face, we're saved by grace,
For on the cross, He took our place.

Abba. Jesus. King of Kings.
Jehovah Jireh gives good things.
He knows His loved ones, each by name.
Once touched by grace, we're not the same.

No pain. No fear. No blame. No shame.
No death. No tears. Hope's found in His name.
The One, True Lord, One God in Three,
Planned all our steps and set us free.

Good news! Let's rise and praise His name.
Christ is the Lord. He stays the same.

Xochitl E. Dixon

50

FROM ME

Many times we write, and the words seem strained, with too much of you and me mixed in. "Don't live up to," Christ says, "But from Me."

So we write from who we are in Christ. When we step out of the way and let Him be our source of strength, He will take our hands and move them to write, and He'll put words on our hearts that speak His truth. He'll send gifts of joy and peace as the words we pen etch lines of hope in the hearts of those who read them.

Christ is worth the time and the death to self that it will take. He is worth the praise those words will give back to Him.

A man who writes books filled with truth once said, "It will cost us much. But we won't miss any of it."

When we give Him our words, He will take them and touch lives in His name.

Bethany Hayes

~ ~ ~ ~ ~ ~

If I waited for perfection...
I would never write a word.

Margaret Atwood

~ ~ ~ ~ ~ ~

51

DAISY DOG

Sweat forms in soft curves as I feel my scare start to slow. My small, black dog, Daisy, lures me from my fast pace on the tile floor. I bend down to pet her head, and thoughts of the note sneak in. Each word brings views of a bride and groom from long past. As I place the note next to the sink and wash my face, tears merge with each splash. I stare at the glass. A grown bride stares back.

Daisy stays close. I pad down the hall and fall into bed. With eyes closed tight, I fake sleep. Daisy curls into my lap and hides. The smooth feel of her soft coat sends warmth right up to my heart. I hear the door and try to slow my breath. But with sure steps, the groom I can't see in the dark stands next to the bed now, with pleas to talk when I feel I can't.

Wind pounds on panes of glass while rain pelts in soft beats with boasts of the sun's rise. Daisy shifts; her warmth in my lap holds me still through the watch of the night as his words pierce the room.

I can't speak. The pause waits with our lives poised on the edge. Is there still room for hope? Or will this be the start of an end?

The walls of the room press in. My lips part but no words form. Daisy tries to soothe with the nudge of her nose. My skin blends with the soft sheet. My groom is gone now. I turn and wait for sleep that just won't come.

Joanne Reese

WHAT I LOVE ABOUT MY CAR

It's not the moon roof I love nor the Bose sound that fills my car. It's more than the easy hatchback and more than the light that glows to warn me of folks in my blind spot. It's yet still more than the switch I flip to "cruise."

I love the front plate on my car. No, I love what's on that plate. And it does its job — to help me find where I've parked and to add joy to those who stop and see it. Once a mom and young girl paused, looked at me at the wheel, and gave me a thumbs up! I smiled both in and out.

The plate shows the "pal" I made out of thick knee socks of grey and white and red. With the right snips and seams and stuff, those socks morphed into thin arms, legs, a trunk, head, ears, and wide mouth.

The best part? Its grin!

My sock friend is not alone; he has friends of his own. My sis sent me sock ear muffs to put on each side (though the heat in my state makes them only fun to look at but never use).

And I like one of my pens best since it has "the sock one" on top. I can say all I ever need to say since it rides the top as I write.

Oh and did I tell you about the rain boots? I say, "Why look grown up when I can wear the boots with my sock friend on all parts?" Rain on the ground is in the way? No worry. Just walk through it.

From the plate, to the pen, to the muffs and the boots — I take great joy in the love I have for my friend made from socks.

Cheryl Lemine

53

THAT'S HOME

Home. What is it? Is it a place far off? A place you left? A place you are now? Home is where roots grow and limbs reach. It's where friends come and hearts go deep. It's where love holds and grace wins. It's where you are free to be you, where you ask God to live, where dreams start and find their end.

But what if home fails? What if the nest falls and the bird is forced to fly? What if the cat sees you and there's no place to hide? God is there. He has wings. He hears chirps of fear and calls for help. He says His ears are perked just for this sort of cry. He likes to scoop up those who know they are small. He winks and says, "Watch this."

Skies part. Clouds run. Rays dart as God speeds to save. "This one is Mine!" He says. The frail soul feels raised, free — whisked away to realms of safe care and sure rest where growth lacks fear and wings reach flight.

Here, in God's heart, home is real. While earth's nests may fall and cats prowl, in our place on high the hearth is warm and the fire sings in joy. Oh to live here! To dwell for all time and more in the sweet care of Christ. To feast, to work, to rest, to fly.

To know you can count on true love — that's home.

Christi Naler

54

MY SPANISH VOICE

My Spanish voice is a bridge. God wouldn't give it to me for no cause at all. It's meant to be used to send those of my house into His house. We speak, read, and write what He asks. We are at His will with our words, our speech, and our time, and we ought to use these well for His cause. Thus, it should be seen that we are not strange, just that we speak two tongues. We're bridging the gap that is lost when we need to be found.

God loves all the lands and those who live far away. We couldn't let time pass us by ere we've shared the Word of God with those who seek His face and His love. What a name we have in Jesus! What love to be called His! What joy to find those who look like me in His house!

Thou art not sent to a people of a strange speech and of a hard language, but to the house of Israel (Ezekiel 3:5 KJV). My Spanish is a way to tell those who speak that tongue to love the Lord with all their hearts, all their souls, and all their minds. This is the way God wants it: that we spread the gospel to all the lands and to all those who need to be saved from their sins by grace in Jesus Christ. How else will the work of the Lord grow if not by our wills to serve put into speech?

*If any man speak in an unknown tongue, let it be by two,
or at the most by three, and that by course; and let one interpret.*

1 Corinthians 14:27 NIV

Erendira Ramirez-Ortega

A STITCH IN TIME

The girl next door rang our bell each day to chat and share a grin or a hug. She was nine years old when she asked me to teach her to sew. She drew a line house and a girl to stitch. She learned to thread three strands and back stitch each line.

"Some folks are messed up," she said. "When I grow up, my life will not be like that." She worked the threads to frame some sense for her life. "I will stay in school and learn to teach and help some kids like me." Her stitch in time saved age nine. How could she know how much her hopes taught me?

The trust of one small girl was God's Show-and-Tell for me that year. If I will let God guide my hands and shape my life, God will make me whole and lead me on. God's stitch in time saves us.

Nancy Reenders

~ ~ ~ ~ ~ ~

I have only made this letter longer because
I have not had the time to make it shorter.

Blaise Pascal

~ ~ ~ ~ ~ ~

56

PROUD

The bus sat in the gray night as each young man took his place in line. Each wore a large pack on his back. Each held a gun at his side. My heart sank to my toes as my son's eyes met mine. Soon he would board the bus and find his seat.

Later — and for a long time — my hands would not touch him nor my ears hear his voice. But I held our last hug deep in my heart. And I didn't wait to pray for God to place His hand on my son's mind, frame, and soul.

My son was to go to war. I was sad, but I didn't faint — for I would trust in the Lord to keep him safe and bring him home.

My son is one of the few and the brave.

I am the proud.

Shelley Pierce

~ ~ ~ ~ ~ ~

It's none of their business
that you have to learn how to write.
Let them think you were born that way.

Ernest Hemingway

~ ~ ~ ~ ~ ~

57

My Hair Is Blue

My hair is blue, like my mood. Sad.

Beeps ring out. Tubes in his mouth. Breaths not his own. Fear fills me. My love is sick. His skin is cold. He is gray, like paste.

Blood hangs red in dark bags at his side — a bit more of life, but will it count? Will he die, all the same?

They say he will.

No hope.

But my tears dwell in God's love like gold flecks that float in the rays of the sun, then fall to the floor. They are more than my sleeve can catch.

I pray Psalms 121: *From where does my help come? My help comes from the LORD.* (ESV) The nurse runs through the room. Fast. Like fire.

She speaks no words.

The test shows a change, for the good. His heart calms.

It seems that he will live, but how can this be? The nurse can't say. Her face is blank. In her world of facts, sans faith, it can't add up. It won't add up.

But I know why his heart grows strong. The Lord felt my tears. My cries fell on ears that hear. God's hands held my love. He gave my young love the chance to grow to be an older man, well and whole. New.

We live in His grace and give thanks for His cure. In God, we thrive. His grace is more than I could earn.

My hair is still blue, but now for the sky, and the day my love did not die.

Leah Hinton

It Makes Sense

At the very first, God made the earth and the sky. How cool is that? He was there before all that we know. He made and takes care of the birds and the trees. In spite of His great size and power, He cares about each one of us. It is a joy to know that the God who made all things takes care of you and me. It makes no sense that He should care about even the day-to-day facts of my life, but He does.

This point of view is the deep-down core of my being and the way I see life and the world. Since God did make us, He must know what is best for us. But even though He also wants the best for each one of us, He gives us the choice to live for Him or not. He didn't have to do that. Since I know that the God who made all things cares about me, it makes sense to live my life for Him.

Grant Showalter

~ ~ ~ ~ ~ ~

Child, to say the very thing you really mean,
the whole of it, nothing more or less
or other than what you really mean;
that's the whole art and joy of words.

C.S. Lewis

~ ~ ~ ~ ~ ~

WHEN I WALK

Mile after mile, bright blue Nike's or ugly brown boots hug my feet and give life to my walks. I try to make tracks every day from my house to town and back. New sounds and smells greet me when spring's song breaks out, when the sun's rays make porch steps so hot that Satan wants a fan, when orange and red leaves are piled high then burned, and when birds fly south. If I am not at home, I find a place to walk.

My treks began 20 years ago after Oprah told me that good change could come with walks. Knees pulled up to my chin, I leaned back on the end of my bed and viewed her proof through tears. I was all about change. My heart had been torn apart, and I think God used that TV show to give me a focus that pulled me from the grip of grief.

On that day, Oprah told all of us that we had to set a pace that wouldn't let us walk and talk at the same time. From then on I have walked on streets from Ohio to Washington, D.C., and from Florida to the San Francisco Bridge where one day I made up my mind to walk its 13.1 miles. I did that four months ago and have my "Look what I did!" medal to prove it. While I walk, I think; I also pray. I tune in to what I hear, and I give thanks for change that comes one step at a time.

Nicey T. Eller

60

WHEN THE DARK BREAKS

When my boy, Jack, was two, he faded away from me. He drew back, locked deep in the vault of his mind, and all his words were locked up too. No more big-cheeked smiles. No laugh to break the dark. No eye gaze. No sweet hugs. Cut off.

Gone. Tall trees and shiny spoons stole his eyes from mine, and I was left with a boy I did not know.

He grew older, and I grew sad.

My heart said, "Don't give up," but I had no idea how to reach him. For years I groped along and found ways to sneak those smiles from the vault. At times a laugh would slip out too, and bring the sun. God put those ways in plain sight for me, I know. Over and over I asked Him to heal Jack's mind, but He chose to bind his heart to mine. We played. We sang. We laughed. We chased, over, and over, and over again.

Jack is nine now, and he steals my heart in ways that may seem strange to most moms. When other boys like him can't bear to be touched or hugged, and most nine-year-old boys would run from their mama's arms, Jack now longs to be held close.

When he grabs my hand first, my mama heart thrills at this. If he looks me in the eyes, I want time to stand still so we can keep this sweet bond. I stare into his soul gates. My heart screams to know my boy. What does his mind keep trapped in that vault? I look at him long after he turns away, back in his own world.

Who are you really, My Love? What does your heart want me to know about you, about your hopes, and about your dreams? Do you think about the next years? I don't think you do. Are you just glad to be here with me today? Yes, I like that too.

The next years scare me more than I can say, but not so much now that we know each other a bit. Now, with hard work, I can fish a few words out of him. He uses lines from *Cars 2* and other kid films, a few words to tell me what he needs. Then, too, I guess and fill in many blanks. I put words in his mouth when he can't and hope they match his thoughts. I pick up tiny crumbs of what he's like, what he wants, what he needs, and how he feels. At times I sift those crumbs for a month or more, until I see a new part of him I have never seen before.

When, with great strain, Jack picks the lock on his word vault to say, "Wuv… you…Mama," my heart melts. I know those words cost him so much work to press out of his mouth. Most of his words still stay trapped in the vault, but his love seeps through the cracks, and that boy can laugh the sun into a dark room like no one else I know.

Sara Hague

~ ~ ~ ~ ~ ~

An essential element for good writing
is a good ear:
One must listen to the sound
of one's own prose.

Barbara Tuchman

~ ~ ~ ~ ~ ~

61

GET A GOOD LIFE!

As one with white hair and age spots, I see that a child of this day isn't like those I grew up with seventy-five years ago. In the place of hands and legs, thumbs are now the most used part of the body. (Guess I shouldn't even write about the spot we all sit on.) Drawn into the noise of fierce games, these kids are in a world known only to them. None of them will ever guide a plow. None will ever pick a bean. None will ever milk a cow. How about climb a tree? Mud pies…huh? Sweat is a thing of the past.

In this day of a busy must-do-this-now mind set, how can I help? Time is the best gift I can give to my young one. With that one, I can spend hours in shared deeds whose aim is a vital life — a life with worth and, best of all, love.

The Holy Bible says that a child must be taught sound rules. This is the chief charge of a grown man or woman who has "been there." Christ's life is the guide to use, and I am asked to help.

Young feet must be led to a right life. What is a right life?

- Faith in God through Jesus Christ. (To grow up into Jesus in all things.)
- Hide words found in the Holy Bible in the heart. Be taught and abide by these words.
- Know and be led by the still, small voice of the Holy Spirit. Don't give place to the Devil.
- Test and chew on the words of those who lead in what is right.
- Rest and feed on food, joy, and love at the Father's table.
- Be kind to all and give to those in want.

My duty as the older adult.

- Live my life as a guide as best I can.
- Speak the truth in love.
- Be in my young one's life.
- Know that one can fail and ask for God's mercy to cleanse a fault or sin.
- Teach a way of life that is good and holy.
- Show a child that a bit of sweat will not bring harm.

Light the path to this other world…the one Jesus fills.

Reba Rhyne

I learned that you should feel when writing,
not like Lord Byron on a mountain top, but
like a child stringing beads in kindergarten
– happy, absorbed and quietly putting
one bead on after another.

Brenda Ueland

62

It Stuns Me

How we have the nerve to turn our backs on God can keep me up at night — the way we scorn Him in what we say, do, and think. The Bible says He cares for us, wants to speak to us and be with us. In *spite* of us.

That stuns me.

Why would He give us a thought? Who of us is worth His time? What in us makes Him stay with us?

The reply must be big. It must be *huge*.

He sent Jesus to earth — God in the flesh — for thirty-three years. Jesus lived with those who spit on Him, chose to hate Him, and in the end, put Him on a cross. To end His life, they pierced Him with a spear, broke His heart. The guards at the foot of the cross split up His clothes (as if they could be worth a dime if He weren't in them).

How did He make them pay for the pain they caused Him?

(This stuns me more.)

Jesus rose from the grave, walked near those who had nailed Him to the tree, who had thought Him not worth the time of day, to tell them this: "If you trust me and make me Lord, a new life is yours. You can laugh at death's sting and live with me in Heaven."

So why would He give all for us? The reply *is* big. No, *huge*.

Love. That's the whole ball of wax.

Does it make sense? No. But how I give thanks for it!

Oh, and it means a good night's sleep, too.

Colleen Shine Phillips

63

COME HOME

Home. I thought it was the last stop of a trip. While I like the chance to see a new place and take in all the sights and sounds (and food) there, I like even more to end a trip where I find the most charm and peace — my home. From a young age, I have loved to go home.

Then I learned that home is not just a house, but it is where my loved ones are. My mom, my dad, my friends. Where they are — that's home, the place we go to meet, talk, laugh, and just be. They have changed my life for good. I love to come home to them.

As I came to know God, *Home* has grown to mean so much more to me. The Word of God tells us that God comes to live in the one who loves the Lord and keeps His Word (John 14:23). God stays with him or her. For good. And for much good. To know God is to find what life is all about. To know God is to find the One who loves us and stays with us through all of time — through each storm and each joy. I love to call God my *Home*.

Now that I am older, I know that home is not just a place; it's a way of life. It's the choice to put God first and keep His ways, to love Him and make Him known. It's the choice to love the ones near us, so they can know God too. *Home* is a way to think, feel, and live. It's a state of mind. We take *home* with us each place we go.

Have you found your home? The place where you find peace and charm? The loved ones who make your heart feel loved? The God who will never leave you? Find your home in Him, and trust Him for the place and the souls to love. Come home.

Katy Kauffman

64

SMOKE

I love smoke. Yes, the death-stick type. I know I am not meant to love a thing that is death. But, I love the smell of smoke. I love the taste. I love the story it tells but not the feel of it when I breathe in.

Now, just so you know, I also love the smell of cut grass, the air after a rain, and a child in my arms. I love the smell of my wife and the smell of the grace that God shares in all that is life.

But, I must say that there is a grip on my soul when I smell smoke. I find a pause in my step. I wait with hope that it may come my way as I watch one who is still in its grip dive into its depth.

I never could grasp the power of a scent until I smelled smoke. It seeps into me like a warm night. It takes me away to a place that I can't see, that I can't hold, and that I can't share with you. It bares my soul. Smoke tells the story that I know how to fail, how to fall, how to be low. It tells the story of a man who was lost, a man who — in the midst of his fall — chose to draw death close to his side.

Yet, even in this deep, dark cave of smoke God is still King. He is King of Kings over death and over smoke. He is the King of hope, the King who came to seek and save the lost, the King who came to bring peace to those who could not find a way home. He is the King of a man whose fall is now but a wisp of smoke in the wind.

He brought me up out of the pit of destruction, out of the miry clay,
and He set my feet upon a rock making my footsteps firm.
Psalm 40:2 NASB

Paul A. Hinton

In Pursuit of a Vision

I spy the dream.

Then doubts mount up.

Should I do it? Was it real?

I take the first step, then the next.

I see the path ahead, but will I get there?

A *yes* here, a *no* there, but I move on.

A force pulls me; I must get to the end.

Now I can't look back; I've come too far.

I see proof that the dream will be real.

More proof pushes me on.

And then, the day is here.

The plan has come true.

Yes, the dream was real.

Marilyn Turk

LOVE BEARS ALL

On one of my many school trips, hubby James and I ran into a fuzzy guy I dubbed "William the Bear." William sports a pin-stripe suit just like the one my man wears to church. From then on, William, also known as my James bear, was packed in my bag for every trip. That way, I could take a part of the love of my life every place I went. At that point, I didn't I know how dear this bear would become.

In 2012 my health was so poor that my man had to feed me, and I thought I was off to Glory. When bad things start, some men flee, but mine stood right by me. In a true test of love, James took care of me and did all chores, plus his job each day. The bear sat by me, so I would know every day what Paul wrote in First Corinthians 13:4-7: *Love suffers long and is kind... bears all things, believes all things, hopes all things, endures all things.* (NKJV)

I believe with all my heart that God will heal. It is a long, hard road to walk, and I lean on God each day. As I face what the day will bring, I smile and thank God for the faith and love of the man I wed 36 years ago. I also hug my James bear as I think, *Love bears all.*

Toby Ann K. Williams

MIND PAIN IS LIFE PAIN

Some have it. Some live it. Some see it. Some are blind to it.

For too many, the mind can fool the self and scare those who are close. They feel that no one sees them. No one cares. No one loves. No one needs them. Their deep cries are not heard, so they learn to stay mute. Or, they lash out. If this is you, don't be scared to reach out. Help can be found. Don't give up!

If you live it, through one you know or love, you are not rare. Don't turn your back. Seek groups for prayer. Find friends who know this pain. They are close if you look.

Read books to learn. Talk to those who teach. Find a doc who cares. Get rest to clear your mind and build your strength for the fray.

If you see it, reach out to help a sick mind in pain, or aid the ones who lift the load. Learn what to do. Ask what he or she needs and try to give it.

Hear. Go slow. Take time. Ask those who know.

Talk to God. Learn how He wants you to show His love.

If you are blind to mind pain in your world, lift your eyes and heart to see the truth. Grow in what you know. Help where you can. Don't close your eyes to this.

Let's work as one to make the world a good place, a safe place, for those who have mind pain.

Cynthia Wheaton

FLUTE IN SMALL BITES

I breathe in God, lift the flute, and hear His voice on the wind. I sense God's gifts to me. I may hear the depth of His love or the breadth of His joy, His wise grace or His soft peace. The sound can calm my soul or lift me to His throne, thrill my heart or bring light joy. I hear His name on every note; I soar on the wings of every tone. I have been known to weep when I play.

It is not I who plays, but He. Do you hear Him too?

Cordie Traber

~ ~ ~ ~ ~ ~

The true alchemists do not change lead into gold; they change the world into words.

William H. Gass

~ ~ ~ ~ ~ ~

WORDS FROM THE WELL

I love to write. I don't write all my thoughts, of course, but when they seem sharp or deep, I grab a pen or click the keys to seize this new thought. Pens and keys catch words and put them in their place. Words halt time so folks can read thoughts not yet theirs. I pray that what I write is worth the pause.

To my grief, I've found that the drive to lock down thoughts will creep into as much of life as I'll let it. At times, my best sense tells me it's crept too far. The urge to keep thoughts can soak up too much "now" space.

I seek to know God and to write Truths to help make God known. One truth is that God must reign above all else. Dare I face the fact that the love to write can turn into a god that keeps me from the one true God who is to be my first love?

What comes from my pen strokes and key clicks must first come from time spent with God and His search of my heart. My words should be drawn from the well where I've sat with God. Ezra 7:10 has long been my goal and my guide: *Ezra had set his heart to study the law of the Lord, and to do it, and to teach the statutes and ordinances in Israel.* (NRSV)

Lord, may no love that is not You take first place in our lives today. Amen.

Margery Kisby Warder

ABOUT THE AUTHORS

Sandy Aletraris grew up in Norfolk, Nebraska and moved to Georgia in 2001. She and her husband reside in Peachtree City. They have three children and nine grandchildren.

They enjoy traveling, and spending time with their children's families.

Sandy is a retired Sr. Coordinator in Chick-fil-A, Inc.'s training department, a Certified Life Coach, and is DISC Certified. Her passion is to encourage and equip others with God's Word to help them navigate their journey in life, especially through the storms they encounter along the way. She is writing a book about how to be an overcomer in the aftermath of a suicide.

Karen O. Allen loves ministry and missions. She lives in Birmingham, Alabama with her husband, George Parker, and two energetic Irish setters.

Karen earned a B.S. in Medical Technology from the University of Southern Mississippi and a Master's in Education from the University of Alabama at Birmingham.

Most of her career has been spent in a hospital or academic healthcare environment. She is a certified clinical research professional in the UAB Comprehensive Cancer Center.

In 2003 Karen was diagnosed with breast cancer which inspired her book *Confronting Cancer with Faith*. Now living a full and healthy life, she glorifies God through her music, motivational speaking, and by writing to encourage others facing crises. She has published devotionals and articles through LifeWay Christian Resources and *The Birmingham Christian Family* magazine as well as other Christian publications.

Sharon Atwood is originally from a small farm town in Hayden, Alabama. She earned a bachelor's degree in Language Arts Secondary Education at Birmingham Southern College, her Master's in Special Education at the University of Alabama at Birmingham, and later became a certified Home Health Aide.

She is employed by the National Alliance of Mental Illness. In addition she volunteers with MPower Ministries preparing low-income adults with challenges to earn their GED.

She immerses herself in poetry, writing, and artistic expressions. An active member of her local church, she enjoys participating in Bible studies in community settings.

At the end of the day Sharon curls up with her special baby cat, Kala Faith.

Kathleen Brown is a writer, speaker, and the author of *A Time for Miracles: Finding Your Way through the Wilderness of Alzheimer's*. She lives and works in the Hill Country of her native Texas and also on the eastern slopes of the Colorado Rockies. She and her husband Harold have three sons and seven grandchildren. You can reach Kathleen at her blog address alzheimershopeandhelp.wordpress.com, or by email: kbrown.writer@google.com.

Kay Camenisch never dreamed of being a writer. She published her first book after her 60th birthday. At the Blue Ridge Mountains Christian Writers Conference, the short writing assignment published in this book helped her realize the importance of writing simply and succinctly.

She felt inadequate, but writing is her passion, and fortunately late starts and feelings of inadequacy can be overcome. She learned from it and honed her writing skills.

Kay has since published three books: *Uprooting Anger: Destroying the Monster Within, The Judgment Trap,* and *The Great Exchange: Bound by Blood,* co-written with her husband, Robert.

Writing helps her fulfill her goal of seeing people grow in the Lord and in harmony with one another. Learn more at randkcamenisch.com.

Ellen Cardwell has been published in *The Upper Room Magazine, Heavenly Company: Entertaining Angels Unaware, Journeys to Mother Love,* several *Inspire* anthologies, *El Dorado Hills Telegraph,* and *Around Here Magazine.* Her first book, *American Proverbs,* was published in 2017 and is available through Amazon.

Larry Cheeves was born in Los Angeles to parents, Lyndell and Dorothy. Lyndell was a lifelong preacher, and both were teachers and educators at the college level.

Growing up in Southern California, Larry graduated from Palm Springs High School. He received a BA in History from Pepperdine University and a Master of Public Administration degree from California State University, Fullerton.

He made his career in city government and served nearly 40 years in five California cities. Larry retired from his last position as City Manager of Union City, California at the end of 2014. He also served for 20 years as an elder in the Church of Christ of Fremont, California.

Larry and his wife of 40 years, Lori, now reside in Camarillo, California where they live close enough to regularly see their two daughters and sons-in-law, and four grandchildren.

Kae Childs teaches the Carolina Shag, the South Carolina state dance, at the University of South Carolina. She has written a book entitled *Life Is a Dance, But Who Is Going to Lead*. She speaks for Stonecroft Ministries, a worldwide Christian organization. Kae is the mother of two and grandmother of four. She is a retired counselor with Charleston County Schools, a tennis and golf enthusiast, and active member of

Seacoast Church. She splits her time between her home on the Isle of Palms which is outside Charleston, and Greenville, South Carolina.

Karen Condit enjoyed a 25-year career as a Reading Specialist and is now pursuing her passion by writing for children. She especially loves testing her stories on her six grandchildren.

She also writes spiritual memoir. Her latest project combines these interests in a series of short stories for children, with themes drawn from the disciplines of the spiritual life. When not writing she enjoys gardening, kayaking, quilting, and connecting with friends for meaningful conversation — always with a good laugh, coffee, and chocolate.

Troy Dennis is an ordained minister and chaplain in Manitoba, Canada. Married to Jan since 1990, they have two grown children.

Troy loves anything to do with the outdoors, including canoeing, photography, hunting, camping, and running. Also musical, he sings and plays trumpet, bass, and acoustic guitar. He and Jan sometimes lead worship together in their home church.

Rosie DiBianca, M.Div. is an ordained pastor. She has served as the Pastor of Discipleship at Bel Air Presbyterian Church in Los Angeles, California and speaks at women's retreats. She has two young adult children and lives in Santa Clarita, California.

Dolly Dickinson graduated from Moody Bible Institute (missions) and Southern Illinois University (philosophy). She worked in publishing many years, writing, editing, and ghostwriting. In 2000 her book *Moving On*, a devotional about coping with divorce, was published. In 2013 it was revised and expanded as an ebook for Kindle. She is retired from working in social services with troubled youth and the mentally ill but keeps just

as busy volunteering at the public library, leading a Divorce Care support group, and filling Operation Christmas Child shoeboxes. Her other interests include her grandchildren, gardening and travel.

Dr. W. Alan Dixon, Sr. lives in Northern California with his best friend, his wife Xochitl. He has two adult sons, AJ and Xavier, a daughter-in-law, Mallory, and a doggy daughter, Jazzy.

Dr. Dixon's passion is to equip leaders with practical tools to help make them successful. Fueled with a desire for learning, he continually works to develop organizational leadership programs for secular and ministry use. He also spends

his time writing articles and devotions to encourage new leaders.

By using his 34 years of leadership experience, Dr. Dixon helps each new leader develop the skills necessary to win in the workplace and in ministry. He is excited about how training and experience coalesce to help make good leaders great and great leaders extraordinary. Join him in this leadership journey as he prepares the leaders who will build the future. LinkedIn: https://www.linkedin.com/in/mralandixon. Twitter:@mralandixon

Xochitl (so-cheel) **E. Dixon** encourages women and teens to embrace God's grace and grow deeper in their personal relationships with Christ and others. She serves as a writer for Our Daily Bread Ministries and as Inspire Christian Writer's Blog and Social Media Director. Married to her best friend since 1994, she enjoys photography, being a wife and mom, traveling, and sharing God's Word through Facebook, Twitter, LinkedIn, and her blog www.xedixon.com.

Nicey T. Eller grew up in the Florida Panhandle and decided she wanted to be a writer. She received her B.A. in English from Shorter College, her M.S. in Secondary Education, and her Ed.S. in Educational Leadership from Troy University.

When she retired as an elementary school principal, she traded her suits for boots, built a log home with her husband, and started a cattle ranch.

Her poetry, inspired by teachers, has been published in *Teachers of Vision* magazine. She was a co-author of *The Mighty Pen (Christian Encouragement from Writers to Writers)*. She serves as a Sunday School teacher and leader in Celebrate Recovery. She is avid reader, walker, and letter writer. Her contact information is nicey.eller123@gmail.com and facebook.com/nicey.eller.

Linda Finlin summarizes her life as seasons for family, education, and personal purpose. The seasons have played out in Texas, California, and Alabama. At nine she became a daughter of the King and loves this spiritual identity.

Linda was a stay-at-home mom until her youngest was in the 4th grade. She attended Midwestern State University, graduating with a BBA, and also attained a CPA license.

She is a grandmother to three.

As a lifetime student, she continues to mine the Word of God through personal study. She leads women's Bible studies and communicates through writing and public speaking.

Sharon Fincannon married Mark Fincannon, a man of God and casting director in the film industry, in 2009. God then opened the door for her to minister to women in that industry. The impact of those encounters continues to be life changing.

God healed, redeemed, and purposed Sharon's previous pain and struggles in her life for the good of others. She's been bringing those treasures to others for several years now by offering wisdom, healing, encouragement, and purpose, in order to help them fulfill their God-ordained destinies. She counts it a great privilege to work with God in having a front-row seat to watch what only He can do in their lives.

One of Sharon's faith-filled experiences is having been diagnosed and miraculously healed of breast cancer in 2013. Her blog, *Moments With Me*, was birthed out of that experience and can be found at momentswithmeblog.wordpress.com.

Anne Grant lives in South Carolina with her husband. She has been active in her church and Bible Study Fellowship. She has four children and seven grandchildren and loves writing, playing the piano, and spending time at the coast.

Joleen Graumann believes everyone was created with purpose and loves inspiring that hope by creating an environment where people can connect with God through worship, a drama, the written Word, or over a cup of tea. A certified coach, she gives seminars on team building by using the *Leading from Your Strengths* personality profile. She enjoys speaking in classrooms and teaching writing workshops to young people.

A native Californian, she resides in the Seattle area with her husband and three young children. Visit her online at: www.joleengraumann.com or www.facebook.com/discovermystrengths to connect about writing.

Annette Griffin is a member of American Christian Fiction Writers, is on the Board of Directors of The Creative Writing Institute, and is writing a historical fiction romance using an allegorical style to make Christ the hero of the story. She and her husband John have five children; three have flown the coop and two 12-year-olds are still at home.

Pamela Groves' childhood helped prepare her for teaching, adopting children and writing, because that's when God taught her that every life is different.

She and her husband married four months after they met, and eventually adopted six children, four with special needs. Their life was a little offbeat with unexpected twists and turns, including his death as age 62 from a rare form of cancer. Through it all, various types of writing and occasional publication have been a part of her life.

Sara Hague is a children's pastor, happy wife, and homeschooling mother of five children including one on the severe end of the Autism Spectrum. A life-long lover of learning, she spends her days brushing up on her geometry and creating lessons for the children in her local church. She has published articles in *Focus on the Family Magazine, Clubhouse Jr.,* and *Christian News Northwest.* She and her family enjoy exploring the area around their home in Central Oregon.

Bethany Hayes, devotional writer, Bible teacher, and lover of the One who first loved her, lives in Gresham, Oregon. She is a member of Oregon Christian Writers. She writes inspirational posts at her blog, www.CapacityCorner.blogspot.com.

Paul Aaron Hinton is the son of a proper British mother and a Mississippi mud father. Never sure if he should aspire to be James Bond or a character from *Hee Haw*, he has worked in many "fields." He hopes his colorful — if not ADD — view of the world reaches those who have never been sure if God needs them. His motto is Philippians 4:13: *I can do all things through Christ who strengthens me.*

Paul has served in the Methodist church for over 20 years as a Lay Minister in both youth and contemporary worship. He and his wife Cecily have three children, plus a "Crazy Cat Lady" starter pack of four cats, and two very big dogs.

Leah "LM" Hinton likes to keep her nose in a book whether she's reading one or writing one.

She also drinks too much coffee.

Married to a detective for over 20 years, she lives in Dallas, has three children — two biological and one adopted — four dogs, a bird, and a horse.

A country girl at heart, this homeschool mom and cancer wife, loves sharing her struggles and blessings with others going through similar situations and firmly believes faith is the best remedy for life's toils.

Doris Hoover lives in Florida, but she also spends time along the coast of Maine. Her passion is discovering God's messages in nature and sharing them with others.

She's won awards for her devotionals and has been published in several compilations and magazines. *Quiet Moments in The Villages, A Treasure Hunt Devotional* is her first book.

Penny L. Hunt is an Amazon.com bestselling author, speaker, devotions writer, and host of the weekly on-line "A Thought from Penny."

The wife of a retired naval officer and attaché, Penny is a grateful grandma, happily living among the peach orchards of rural South Carolina with her husband Bill, and two rescue pups.

Learn more about Penny at her website www.PennyL.Hunt.com.

Tina Hunt is an encouraging communicator, whether writing or speaking. By day she pastors a congregation in the Church of the Brethren, and most evenings you'll find her caring for her grandson. She has served as Co-President of Word Weavers Northeast Ohio and a mentor in Word Weavers International. You can find her reflections and devotions on her blog, https://potofmanna. wordpress.com, or on the writers' website: www.almostanauthor.com.

Rev. Dr. Cureton L. Johnson has been pastor at the First Baptist Church Moore Street in Fayetteville, North Carolina, for 26 years. He previously served as the Outreach Director for the Christian anti-hunger organization, Bread for the World, in Washington, D.C. He has received awards from the NC General Assembly for hosting HIV/AIDS Sunday worship services and from the Fayetteville Quaker House for his "Prophetic Voice" in the peace movement.

Dr. Johnson is the author of *Alligator Courage*, and is a former editor of the *Baptist Informer* newspaper. A UNC-Chapel Hill graduate in journalism, Pastor Johnson holds the MDiv degree from Shaw Divinity School (Raleigh) and the DMin degree from Drew University (New Jersey). He has traveled on missions to Guyana, Kenya, Zimbabwe, and Zambia. He is married to Lena Goode-Johnson and they have two children and two grandchildren. cjohnson@1st-baptist.com

Katy Kauffman is a Bible teacher, an award-winning author, and a co-founder of Lighthouse Bible Studies. She is an editor and a designer of *Refresh Bible Study Magazine*. She is also the designer of *Broken but Priceless: The Magazine*. Her Bible studies for women focus on winning life's spiritual battles. Katy loves spending time with family and friends, finding the best decaf coffee, and making jewelry. Connect with her at http://lighthousebiblestudies.com.

Rich Kehoe has a Master of Arts Degree in Theology from Talbot Theological Seminary and over 35 years of experience in large evangelical churches leading couples' groups in spiritual growth and discipling men. He has published a book titled *Transforming Love – Growing in Intimacy with God.* He is the Executive Director of Journey into Light. He also maintains a website and blog at http://journeyintolight.info that provides

information and practical ways to grow in intimacy with God.

He came to Christ and was discipled and trained for ministry for six years by the Navigators. He has an Industrial Engineering degree and an MBA. He is retired from a career in administrative services for county government. He and his wife, Adele, live in Highland, California. They have a daughter, a son and daughter-in-law, and three grandchildren.

Liz Kimmel lives in St. Paul, Minnesota, has been married for 38 years, and is the mother of two and grandmother of four.

She earned a BA in Elementary Education at Bethel College in Arden Hills, Minnesota. She writes for and is layout editor for her bi-monthly church publication.

She has published two books of Christian poetry and loves to write in such a way as to make learning fun for elementary students.

She has published a grammar workbook; her current project is a set of worksheets about the 50 States, created in order of statehood, and incorporating math and language arts skills in addition to lots of puzzles. Liz currently serves as the Communications Coordinator for Bethel Christian Fellowship, in St. Paul.

Marilyn Klunder has been an Indiana elementary educator for four years. She is a passionate teacher who also enjoys writing about her personal faith experiences. She uses her writings as devotions, Bible study topics, and to encourage and teach others. She is working on a personal reflection based upon changing uniforms in God's army; how she's gone from wearing a humble white robe to a fully-armored warrior with sword (the Word of God) drawn.

Marilyn resides in Kouts, Indiana, with Neil, her husband of 16 years. Together they have six children and eight grandchildren.

Margaret Lalich is a teacher, blogger, and speaker. She is also a believer, lover — of family, friends, and others — a relentless optimist, and a Certified Laughter Leader.

She's a mid-life career-changer who left retail management to become a college freshman at age 36. She has since completed graduate school with a Master of Arts in Education (Special Education), and a Master of Science in Speech-Language Pathology.

She says she is a perfect example of how far God can move a one-time high-school dropout very far! She knows it's never too late or too hard for God to make miracles of our lives.

Margaret is 73 years young, mother of two, grandmother (or Nana) of eight, great-grandmother of one...and widow of Joseph Lalich — the love of her life — after being blessed with a 45-year-long honeymoon.

Don Lee was busy awarding the coveted finisher medal at the Boston marathon finish line in April 2017; it was his 21st time to volunteer. He has qualified and completed 12 Boston marathons and numerous other marathons, Ironman, and other triathlons.

The retired educator enjoys word play and playing the guitar and banjo. He and his wife live in Northeast Ohio except when visiting their four sons around the country and globe.

Cheryl B. Lemine — a professional writer, sock-monkey collector and gel pen fanatic — lives 17 miles from Jacksonville Beach, Florida.

She's written local community news as well as medical and family-related stories for *The Florida Times-Union, H for Health,* and *First Coast Magazine.*

For the last 10 years, it was her honor to teach creative writing to 6th through 8th graders at LaVilla School of the Arts — a public, magnet middle school in Jacksonville.

Ready to begin a new chapter, she recently resigned to pursue national-magazine writing and start a nonprofit focused on children's literacy. She and her husband live with a domestic shorthair cat and a rescue kitty.

Sarah G. Smith Lewis was born in New Jersey, and raised Presbyterian. She graduated from Bucknell, then taught English and Latin in Manasquan High School until she met and married Methodist minister Rev. Fay H. Smith.

They served churches in New Jersey and Illinois, and spent 12 years in Africa where Sarah used what she'd learned while obtaining her Masters degree in ESL to develop a program for students who wished to study abroad.

After 12 years in Zaire (now the Democratic Republic of Congo) they were assigned to work with United Methodist Men in Nashville, Tennessee, where Sarah began teaching at the International English Institute.

After Fay completed his life journey in 1992, Sarah continued teaching for several years before marrying Dr. Jacob Lewis from New Jersey, thus making a full circle journey of 93 years (so far).

Kimberly Long has a love for many things, but writing, photography, cooking, mountain biking, and spending time with grand babies are at the top.

Several books have been in her heart and strewn throughout spiral notebooks for years. She finished and published her first book, *Financial Hope,* in 2012. This book recounts a journey from the hardships of living in poverty to the many miracles of walking out of poverty, step by step.

Kimberly considers herself blessed to be living in the Texas Hill Country among amazing friends and awesome church. She continually prays for her kids to heed God's voice to move closer to where she lives.

Eric Mueller is an ex-meth addict who experienced a short stint in jail. He is now an ordained pastor and prison-ministry leader. His unique experiences speak to the thousands he has mentored, discipled, and walked with in this path to life-change.

He is a teacher with Mercy and Grace Ministries' certificate program that partners with Western Seminary.

Uniquely gifted, he has a passion to help move mountains in people's lives by revealing Biblical truths with a new perspective. Eric is married and has a one child — of the canine variety, that is.

Alice H. Murray lives in Florida, where she has practiced adoption law (domestic non-related infant adoptions) for over 25 years. She is an officer and board member of the Florida Adoption Council and of Hope Global Initiative.

While being a lawyer is her profession, her passion is writing. She won a haiku contest for the American Bar Association, has had several law-related articles printed in legal publications, and the story she wrote about her recent mission trip to Ecuador appeared in her local newspaper. She is currently working on two books.

Christi Naler grew up in a suburb, moved to a mini farm for several years, and has travelled extensively around the world. She lives in a tiny house of sorts — a single small bedroom in the Bay Area, complete with a compact kitchen corner doubling as an office.

She enjoys writing, professional organizing, playing the piano, and spending time with her family. She also loves deep conversations, lasting friendships, reading, ethnic foods, foreign films, and all things worship. Her life has been one of much change and finding much grace. She looks forward to opportunities seen and unseen, travel for the purpose of loving and serving the global church, and enjoyment of home in all the variety of forms God gives her.

Suzanne Dodge Nichols grew up in Gulf Breeze, Florida. During high school, she discovered the rewarding discipline of writing. Through the years, she has found creative expression in almost every genre of the printed word.

She enjoys blending words and art in ways that can both delight and challenge the observer.

She leads a scripture memory and Bible skills program for older elementary children. Her many years as program director led her to develop a three-cycle curriculum for older children. More recently, she added a companion curriculum for younger elementary children — a foundational program she named "Bible Basics."

Suzanne makes her home in Hartselle, Alabama with Roger, her husband of 41 years. They have three children and seven grandchildren who live *much* too far away.

Eréndira Ramirez-Ortega's fiction is featured in *Day One, The Cossack Review, The Black Warrior Review, Fourteen Hills, Other Voices, Santa Clara Review,* and *La Calaca Review.* Her book reviews are featured in *Blogging for Books;* her non-fiction is featured in *The Washington Post, Brain, Child Magazine, Huffington Post, Red Tricycle, The Tishman Review, Cordella Magazine, Life in 10 Minutes, Stone Soup Magazine, The Review Review,*  and *Front Porch Commons: A Project of the CLMP.* She has work forthcoming in *West Branch* and *The Sunlight Press.* A homeschool mom and former adjunct, Eréndira lives in Southern California with her husband and three children. She is writing a novel.

Colleen Shine Phillips is passionate about God and ministry. Teaching, leading, and discipling have dominated the last 40 years of her life, and although she still continues with these activities, her primary professional role today is writing. She has authored plays, lessons, Bible studies, articles, and short stories, as well as placing in several writing contests in various genres. You can read her published works of fiction in *Clubhouse,*  Focus on the Family's magazine for middle readers.

She lives with her family in Quilpué, Chile.

Shelley Pierce is a pastor's wife, mom to four, grandmother, and author. Playing with the grandkids is her favorite way to spend a day.

She enjoys her day job, serving as Director of Preschool and Children's Ministries at Towering Oaks Baptist Church in Greeneville, Tennessee.

Her writing includes children's curriculum with *LifeWay Kids*, and a column in *Christian Online Magazine*. She has contributed to *The Upper Room, Power* for *Living, Guideposts The Joys of Christmas, The Mighty Pen,* and *Stupid Moments*.

Shelley chooses to look at the bright side of life, believing that God can be trusted to keep His promises. To her, ifficulties in life — such as a son deployed in a war zone — are all opportunities to grow in faith and depend on God to meet needs.

Pamela K. Proudfoot, a graduate of Lourdes College, has worked in a variety of careers — some of which include cosmetologist, security officer, emergency-medical technician, police and fire dispatcher, safety instructor, police officer, and administrator for the U.S. Census Bureau.

She serves in nursing homes, prison ministry, and missionary outreach to Camarines Northe, Philippines in addition to four trips to Mexico.

Pamela's hobbies include photography and gardening. Her latest focus is writing articles, autobiography, and short stories.

She is the mother of two sons, and grandmother of five grandsons and one granddaughter.

Jennifer Saake is blessed to be Rick Saake's wife. She is thankful for three long-awaited miracle babies here on earth and three more awaiting her in heaven.

She is co-founder and director emeritus of Hannah's Prayer Ministries, offering international support to families facing fertility challenges (Hannah.org), and is the author of *Hannah's Hope: Seeking God's Heart in the Midst of Infertility, Miscarriage, & Adoption*. She hopes to write more books in the near future.

She blogs at *InfertilityMom, Stroke of Grace, and Harvesting Hope*.

In 2011, at age 39 Jenni survived six near-fatal strokes via chiropractic accident. Visit her at Facebook/StrokieGal, and @ InfertilityMom on Pinterest and Twitter.

Nancy Reenders is a graduate of Calvin College with a degree in elementary education. After teaching preschool and raising a family, she served for 20 years as Hunger Response Director at Access of West Michigan.

In retirement Nancy writes creative non-fiction and continues to advocate for social justice.

She lives with her husband, Garry, in Grand Rapids Michigan.

Joanne Reese started life in the beautiful Hudson Valley region of New York where dreams of becoming a figure skater melted into the desire to become a prima ballerina. Nowadays she finds expression through writing.

She launched her writing career with devotions published in *Light from the Word* and on <u>CBN.com</u>. She's had articles published in *The Christian Communicator*, *Light & Life*, *P31 Woman* and *Vista* magazines. She's also written regularly for the *Living Series* magazine in the Central Valley of California.

When she's not busy working part-time at her local library, she enjoys taking long walks, spending time with her family, and commiserating with the protagonist for her next novel. Visit her website: <u>www.JoanneReese.com.</u>

Jane Reid's writing is a life-long habit. By her teens, painful thankful notes grew into chatty letters and daily journaling. She dreamed of writing picture books, poetry, and children's novels, but thought it impossible. She also thought getting married and having children was impossible.

After four years of college and 23 years of home schooling her four children, she's learned nothing is impossible. She led children's music and drama groups for 15 years while taking classes to learn how to do it. She is still busy learning how as she crafts children's novels and devotional meditations for adults.

She is grandmother to eight little ones, all under the age of five. Her husband of over 40 years is her first reader and biggest fan. You can read her work for adults at www.cardinal-sound.com.

Reba Rhyne is the pen name of Reba Carolyn Rhyne Meiller. In high school, reading was a favorite past-time. More than once she heard, "Carolyn, turn off your light and go to sleep," at one o'clock in the morning.

Three-quarters of a century have passed since Reba was born During this time, she was married for 25 years, had a daughter, and established a business of her own.

Writing began as a hobby while she spent months at a time at her customers' locations. She now travels the world for pleasure and business.

For sixty years, she has been a Christ-follower who believes her responsibility is to follow the Great Commission found in Matthew.

She shares fifteen acres in Tennessee with Phil the Groundhog, skunks, possums, rabbits, squirrels, deer, an occasional bear and her cubs, a high-flying hawk, and a bobcat. They get along very well.

Katherine Rice is a wife and business partner with her husband of 35 years. Together they have six grown children and six grandchildren. Katherine spent her years raising children as a homeschool teacher and homemaker. As her children reached adulthood, she began to focus on developing her love of writing, as well as teaching and mentoring young women.

Still very busy with business and family, she now helps support her mother who lives in a nearby memory-care facility.

Driven by the idea that her words may influence someone's life, either now or sometime in the future, Katherine finds that writing brings her great satisfaction.

Ele (Eleanor) Richardson is an 86-year-old retired teacher who spent many years teaching English to adults from around the world. She was married to husband, Niel, for 61 years. She has four children, eight grandchildren, and six great-grandchildren.

Originally from Pittsburgh, Ele now lives in a small red house near Cleveland with two large, affectionate cats.

She is active in her Methodist church and enjoys weaving, playing bells, reading, feeding birds, and finding wildflowers. She loves spending time on Cape Cod and at the John C. Campbell Folk School in North Carolina, where she has taken classes in weaving, dyeing, and beadworking.

In the summer of 2016, Ele was the flower girl at her granddaughter's wedding.

Michelle Ruschman is a wife of Mark and mother of one daughter. They call the Florida Panhandle home.

Michelle loves teaching about essential oils, has a wearable technology business and creating artisan jewelry for her first entrepreneurial venture, Philippine Script Designs. Her jewelry business showcases *baybayin*, the original writing system of the Philippines, but Michelle is best known for Beautifully Broken, her one-of-a-kind dichroic glass crosses.

Because of her busy schedule, Michelle does most of her writing in the middle of the night. She claims it's the only time her mind is finally quiet enough to receive inspiration from the Lord, and she loves the tranquility of those dark hours. Michelle writes mainly for her blog, *The Devotions of a Prodigal Daughter*.

Toni Armstrong Sample retired early to Greenwood, South Carolina at the end of a successful career as a human-resource executive. She has written for professional journals, recreational magazines, devotionals, newspapers, and inspirational-story publications. Her first novel, *The Glass Divider*, was released in 2014 followed in 2015 and 2016 with *Transparent Web of Dreams, Distortion*, and *A Still Small Voice*.

Toni is a Christian retreat leader and conference speaker, Christian education and women's Bible study facilitator and commission artist — concentrating on painting Biblical scenes and characters. Her first non-fiction book, *I'll Never be the Same*, was released in 2017. Her second non-fiction book is titled *A Buck Three Eighty (A Baby-Boomers Stories About Growing Up in the North)*. Future novels include *The Soup Kitchen Gala*, and *The Song of My Soul*. She also has inspirational stories published in the *Moments* series.

Kevin Louise Schaner's upcoming book, *Dinner by Candlelight: Comfort and Joy for Advent*, includes personal essays that encourage conversation. She has traveled to Africa ten times with United Methodist Volunteer in Mission teams. Her articles in *Response Magazine* report on additional relationship-building experiences through United Methodist Women's Ubuntu Journeys to four other continents.

Kevin practices Spanish every day and has recently learned to strum a baritone ukulele. She hikes all four seasons on the North Coast and loves living in multicultural Cleveland Heights, Ohio. Contact her at schanerkevin@gmail.com.

David Alan Shorts is a writer, speaker, and musician from Lodi, California. A graduate of San Jose State's school of music, he has spent the last 18 years teaching elementary music and band. When he's not being a daddy to his three incredible children, he speaks at a convalescent hospital, snow skis, and flies model airplanes.

David wrote his first story, *Melido's Blade*, in sixth grade. In high school he switched to musician mode and pursued a career, playing at local venues and writing many songs and a few musicals. He released two albums under the names *Strohsdivad* and *Dead Poet Clan.*

For the last ten years he has written many YA novels, screen plays, and children's stories. This year he added flash fiction and devotional writing.

Visit his web page at www.facebook.com/DavidAlanShorts.

Grant Showalter has been teaching youth Sunday School at his church for more than 20 years. He believes the entire Bible and thinks it can have a major influence when young people know the Word. Because he believed standard Sunday School curriculum was far too narrow in scope, he found himself digging into the Word to bring a more comprehensive overview to his lessons. That led to *The Minute Bible* audio series, a summary of each book of the Bible in one minute. Grant researched, wrote, and recorded the audio series. He is also a Christian DJ, a Bass player at church, and has recently earned his pilot's license.

Debbie Sprinkle strives to let God take the lead in her writing. She co-authored *Exploring the Faith of America's Presidents*. After she attended the Proverbs 31 Ministry's She Speaks Christian Writers' Conference at the request of the Women's Leader at her church, Debbie became a member of her church's Women's Speaking and Writing Team. She has since written questions for several studies used by the women's group.

In May, 2016, Debbie won first place for an unpublished short story at the Blue Ridge Mountains Christian Writers' Conference. She has since contributed to two anthologies compiled by Collierville Christian Writers' Group. She is currently working on several projects, including three romantic suspense novels.

Cordie Traber loves playing the flute as part of the praise team at Valley Baptist Church in San Rafael, California. She and George, her husband of 30 years, manage rental properties inherited from his parents. She helps with management of the care of her aging parents.

Besides volunteering as Assistant Children's Supervisor for Bible Study Fellowship in Marin County, she gets great pleasure tending her vegetable garden, and trying new gourmet recipes for her husband and guests.

Cordie's mission is to love and serve God and His people with joy and grace. Some days she is better at it than others, but her passion for Jesus Christ, regardless of any difficult circumstances that crop up just in the process of living, is evident to those around her.

Marilyn Turk loves to study history, especially that of lighthouses and the coast of the United States. She is the author of *Rebel Light*, *A Gilded Curse*, and *Lighthouse Devotions – 52 Inspiring Lighthouse Stories*, based on her lighthouse blog, http://pathwayheart.com.

Marilyn has written for publications including *Guideposts* magazine, *A Joyful Heart*, *A Cup of Christmas Cheer*, *Daily Guideposts*, *The Upper Room*, *Clubhouse Jr*. magazine, *Chicken Soup for the Soul*, and *Lighthouse Digest* magazine. She also has written two Christmas plays for her church.

Marilyn lives in Florida with her husband and enjoys boating, fishing, tennis, gardening, climbing lighthouses, and playing with her grandsons. She speaks on a number of subjects, from her stays as caretaker at Little River Lighthouse in Maine, to messages of encouragement. She also teaches workshops on writing and directs the Blue Lake Christian Writers Retreat. Her newsletter is available at marilynturk@pathwayheart.com.

Beverly Varnado is an award winning novelist, screenwriter, and blogger. Her screenplay, *Give My Love to the Chestnut Trees,* has been a finalist for the Kairos Prize and is now under option with Elevating Entertainment Motion Pictures. Her novels are *Home to Currahee* and *Give My Love to the Chestnut Trees*, which placed in the top ten for Christian Writer's Guild Operation First Novel. Her blog, *One Ringing Bell*, is now in its seventh year with almost seven hundred posts. Beverly's work has been featured on World Magazine Radio, *The Upper Room* magazine, and *Southern Distinctions Magazine*. Learn more at www.BeverlyVarnado.com

Margery Kisby Warder, author and speaker, has taught Bible studies, written curriculum, and presented church and community programs. She worked for newspapers before buckling down to complete two novels, an original Christmas collection, a busy woman's "retreat" book, a children's Advent book, and co-authoring devotionals with husband, Paul. Most of their writings are online.

In 2016 her poem about Abraham's journey up Mt. Moriah won first place at OWFI and earned her a 2017 scholarship to Mt. Hermon Christian Writers Conference. Margery hopes that more Christians send online Christian books and short stories as missionaries where Bibles might be refused. To learn more or to contact her, email her at author.speaker4Him@gmail.com or visit https://margerywarder.wordpress.com. The Warders applaud their adult children's ministries, but wish they could spoil their grandchildren more often.

Cynthia Baughan Wheaton earned an MBA from UNC-Chapel Hill at a time when few women sought one. She spent 9 years managing new ventures and over 25 years as a business consultant, while active in church and community.

In 2012, Cynthia established *The Entrepreneur's Friend®*, a website offering practical guidance, encouraging character development, and sharing spiritual insight to help others plan, start, and grow businesses. Her first book, *Are You Ready to Start Your Own Business?,* was released on Amazon.

Cynthia and her husband have nurtured two children into adulthood, while working together from their Chapel Hill home.

Jan White is a wife, mother, and writer. Her articles have been published in *Charisma Magazine, Focus on the Family, CBA Marketplace, Christian Retailing,* and *The Alabama Baptist.*

She has worked for three newspapers and written a weekly religion column for *The Andalusia Star-News* for 23 years. Her column has also been published in *The Southeast Sun* in Enterprise, Alabama for over 10 years.

Kenneth Avon White is an aspiring writer who was first published in *The Upper Room* magazine. Ken's professional background includes work in radio and television advertising, public relations, corporate communications, and most recently, information technology. He dreams of the day when writing is his career; but in the meantime, he is grateful for the clock he punches. Ken currently resides in Nashville, Tennessee and enjoys the local music scene, theatrical shows, and art exhibits. Also high on his list is dining out with a cast of characters — otherwise known as close friends — who have all been warned that most likely they will find themselves in one of his stories someday.

Toby Ann K. Williams married James, her knight in shining armor, and God blessed them with two children. Serving as foster parents, James and Toby adopted a sibling group of three.

With a heart for struggling students, Toby became a teacher at a Christian school and later became a principal. Knowing her students had undiscovered abilities, she worked to inspire them, then watched as they reached unbelievable goals. She now consults with other schools, empowering teachers to teach "all" of God's children.

Toby is a speaker and writer who loves spending time with her grandchildren and enjoys traveling, reading, and walking on the beautiful beaches. Contact her at tobywilliams5@gmail.com.

Joseph Yates grew up in a small town in Mississippi, had a traditional Christian upbringing, and has since worshiped and studied with a number of Christian denominations and spiritual groups.

He attended Ole Miss (the University of Mississippi) under the Regular Navy ROTC program, earned a BA degree, and was commissioned upon graduation. After that, he traveled extensively with the Navy, and is a Vietnam veteran.

Following active duty, he returned to Ole Miss, earned a Master's degree in urban and regional planning, and a doctorate (J.D.) in law. He practiced law, and served in a number of related positions in business and government. He is now semi-retired.

Joseph is member of American Mensa, the National Eagle Scout Association, the Mississippi Bar, and the State Bar of Texas. He lives with his wife, Mary, and two 10-year-old Pomeranians.